Black in School

Kemi Oluyinka
& Caren Onanda

Black in School

The Black Teacher's Guide for Surviving the Classroom

A SAGE Publishing Company

1 Oliver's Yard
55 City Road
London EC1Y 1SP

CORWIN
A Sage company
2455 Teller Road Thousand Oaks
California 91320 (800)233-9936
www.corwin.com

Unit No 323-333, Third Floor, F-Block
International Trade Tower,
Nehru Place, New Delhi – 110 019

8 Marina View Suite 43-053
Asia Square Tower 1
Singapore 018960

Editor: James Clark
Assistant editor: Esosa Otabor
Production editor: Nicola Marshall
Copyeditor: Sharon Cawood
Indexer: C&M Digitals (P) Ltd, Chennai, India
Marketing manager: Dilhara Attygalle
Cover design: Wendy Scott
Typeset by: C&M Digitals (P) Ltd, Chennai, India

Library of Congress Control Number: 2024937109

British Library Cataloguing in Publication data

A catalogue record for this book is available from the British Library

ISBN 978-1-5297-9882-1
ISBN 978-1-5297-9881-4 (pbk)

Contents

About the Authors

Kemi Oluyinka has worked in the education sector for over 10 years. She is a qualified SENCO and science teacher, and has experience as an education consultant. She has held different leadership positions over the last 10 years and was previously an assistant headteacher in London. She started the first four years of her career in mainstream education settings and then moved to an alternative provision for another four years before she decided to work internationally as a science teacher and SENCO in Dubai. Kemi wants to do more in the world of education to support fellow Black teachers and students, especially students from disadvantaged backgrounds. She is the founder of the Black Teachers Network, previously known as the Young Black Teachers Network (YBTN), which was established in 2018. She has been featured on BBC News, in the Huffington Post and Guardian Labs.

Caren Onanda has taught and volunteered across the education sector for over 24 years, from Widening Participation projects with the Universities of Cambridge and York, to work with NAGTY (G&T provision) and at international summer schools. She is passionate about improving the life outcomes of young people, especially those from disadvantaged backgrounds. She has been teaching English in secondary schools in England for 17 years and has held various leadership positions, from Head of Year and Head of Department, to Lead Practitioner, and is now a member of the Senior Leadership Team at her current school. Caren has also embarked upon a Doctorate in Education in order to further explore and research the journeys of Black educators in the UK. She is keen to ensure good practice is shared and strong networks are built and developed across schools in diverse settings. Caren is a Trustee for Southside Young Leaders Academy and on the advisory board for Penguin Lit in Colour. She has written for various educational blogs including Schools' Week. She is the South London Hub lead for the Black Teachers Network.

List of Contributors

Wonu Adedoyin-Salau is an Assistant Headteacher at an East London secondary school and Sixth Form.

Sarah Adenuga is an English teacher and experienced senior leader.

Albert Adeyemi has been a qualified teacher for over five years and is co-founder of Black Men Teach, an education network raising the profile of Black Men in Education.

Kafilat Agboola is a science teacher, MAT Director of Professional Learning and Executive Coach with over 10 years of senior and system leadership experience.

Massimo Ampofo is a Secondary English teacher currently working in a British International school in Dubai.

Grace Anane-Agyei is a co-founder of the education company Xoleio and serves as an examiner for AQA.

Emmanuel Awoyelu is an Educator, SENCO and former Assistant Head Teacher currently working in the Middle East as an Inclusion Specialist Teacher and consultant.

Alessandro Babalola is an Olivier award winning actor, writer, director, musician and dramaturg of Nigerian descent, born and raised in East London.

Genevieve Bent is an Associate Vice Principal, overseeing Post 16, Assessment & Reporting, and Initial Teacher Training.

Olajumoke Champion started her career as a teacher of computer science and Head of Year; after five years in teaching, she changed her career path into project management.

Natalie Cole is the Head of English at a British International School.

Petal Darnley teaches business and economics at a British International School in Dubai.

Helen Debrah-Ampofo is an English teacher from London, now based in the UAE.

Chioma Ezeh is a London-based product designer and storyteller, having worked across theatre and film, both behind and in-front of the camera.

Evelyn Forde MBE is a successful Headteacher, winner of the TES HT of the year award and the first Black female President of ASCL which represents over 24,000 members.

Rhia Gibbs is a consultant and founder of Black Teachers Connect, a global network of Black teachers.

Shani Glover is an Assistant Headteacher in a primary school.

Paige Griffin is an educator with over 10 years' experience working in a range of schools and currently works as a SEND educational consultant.

Damiebi Iteye-Obi has 10 years of experience teaching and is the lead advocate for Black Men in Education for the Black Teachers Network.

Nana-Kofi Okyere is a Senior Lead in a local authority overseeing a SEN team and published author.

Alison Kriel was an inner city Executive Head Teacher for nearly 20 years leading her schools to be in the National top 100 and highest performing in London.

Michaela Lawson is the founder of Building Anti Racist Education (formerly The Prosperity Project), an organisation dedicated to advancing racial literacy in schools.

Adrian McLean is a current Executive Leader and former Head Teacher, an Ambassador of Character Education, Trustee of Governors for Schools, Advisory Board Member for ImpactED and Reach Out 2 Kids.

Seyi Noibi has worked in a variety of different school roles from Deputy Head of Year, Head of Department to now Head of Faculty.

Audrey Pantelis' career in education as a teacher and school leader spans over thirty years; she was the founding Head of a free special school in northwest London.

Daniel Robinson is an Assistant Headteacher serving young people from an inner London community.

Aaron Senessie is a mathematics teacher with over 10 years, teaching experience at state, private, inner London and suburban schools.

Shamila Sulaiman is a UX Consultant. She is also a playwright and director.

Aisha Thomas is a former Assistant Principal and the founder of Representation Matters.

Gradi Tomene is an Assistant Head Teacher in a London secondary school, with over 15 years of experience working with young people.

Bianca Williams is an Associate Assistant Headteacher in a mixed-comprehensive secondary school in inner-London.

Toby Williams has taught primary and secondary and became the youngest Assistant Headteacher in the country. He is now a Learning Operations Manager at an ed tech company.

Amanda Wilson is the Headteacher of a one-form entry primary school in south London and has over 20 years' experience in education.

Acknowledgements

God first, always. I always dreamed of being a published author and it's by the grace of God that this has come to life. To my amazing husband for always listening, advising and being my voice of reason. To my parents for always encouraging me to write since I was a little girl and instilling the value of education in me. You've always believed in me and challenged me to be the best I can be. Thank you for your sacrifices and being the best parents a daughter could ask for. To my family, friends and everyone who has poured into me over the course of my career in education and has always believed in me whenever I say I'm going to do something, even when it sounds unrealistic; your mentorship, coaching, advice, support and prayers have helped me along the way. Last but not least, thank you Adele Bates, for being the connect.

Kemi Oluyinka

I want to say a huge thank you to my family and to all those who have gone before me. I hope we are your wildest dreams! A special thank you to my parents, for all the sacrifices, guidance, leadership, mentoring, coaching, education, support and willingness to go where no one has gone before. Thank you for being such trailblazers for me, Mum and Dad. Thank you for setting the example and being so resilient in the face of untold strife. Thank you for being 'the only Black faces' in countless rooms, so that we would not feel afraid to take the next step(s). Thank you for never running away from the obstacles and challenges that life brought and for showing us how to 'make lemonade' à la Beyoncé! Finally, thank you for your faith in God, in me and in all that I have ever wanted to do. You've never dampened my spirits, or put limits on my dreams. There's still more to come!

Thank you, Seraphina. Because of you, I am.

Last, but by no means least, I thank God. For everything.

Caren Onanda

About the Book

If only there was a manual, a guide that would help me along my teaching journey as a Black Educator in the 21st century.

That's exactly what this book is. Kemi and Caren realised they had similar ideas and had something great in the works when they were on an Inclusive Leadership training course in 2019. They knew something was missing in the world of education and it was this book.

As we become a more diverse society, we must also become more inclusive; the two go hand in hand and they are not tick-box activities. This book is to encourage Black educators who may be facing similar situations in their school settings. However, this book is also for those who are not Black so they can understand the experiences of Black educators, which will help to inform their practices as well as workplace systems. We hope we can foster true, long-lasting change that will create a diverse and inclusive environment that is equitable when it comes to addressing the issues faced by Black members of staff (Haque and Elliott, 2018).

As you read this book, you will hopefully find that there is something for you, or maybe you will see yourself in one of the experiences shared. Perhaps you are evaluating what you do well in your school and how you could improve, to ensure your school is moving in the right direction. We want everyone to learn from this book and to take heed of the words read, as it's the little changes now that will have the greatest impact in the long run: for schools, teachers and the students we teach.

This book has captured the voices of many people who have worked in various roles across decades and throughout England and internationally. Each unique story aims to teach us all a lesson on how we can do and be better; not just for ourselves, but for the future of the education system. There is at least one Big Question at the end of every chapter, as we want everyone reading this book to broaden their horizons and think deeper. Not only do we want you to think, we actually want you to take action and do something with the knowledge you gain. Put together an action plan in order to find a solution and make it a little easier for the next generation of teachers coming into the education sector. Teachers are leaving in droves and the sector is strained with budget cuts. That, as well as the systemic racism Black educators face, means that the challenges faced by us can seem overwhelming. How do we encourage more Black people to choose to become a Black teacher? How do we ensure they stay and they are supported? How do we remove whatever ceilings and barriers there are to ensure they can progress at the same rate as their counterparts? How do we ensure that Black students see themselves in those who teach them? Of course, students can connect with teachers who are not Black, but we cannot ignore the cultural element (Maylor et al., 2006). There are some unspoken matters a Black teacher can understand instantly, that someone who is not will struggle to, or fail to, understand; despite even the best of intentions. How do we ensure that there is growing and sustained representation at all levels within the education sector?

We hope that this book builds on the research, work, studies and lived experienced of all the Black teachers who have come before us. We hope we encourage, sustain, enthuse and lift up all our brothers and sisters. There is strength in union.

A cord of three strands is not easily broken.

(Ecclesiastes 4:12, Christian Standard Bible (CSB))

References

Haque, Z. and Elliott, S. (2018) *Visible and invisible barriers: The impact of racism on BME teachers*. London: National Union of Teachers. Available at: https://neu.org.uk/sites/default/files/2023-02/Barriers%20Report.pdf (accessed 6 March 2024).

Maylor, U., Ross, A., Rollock, N. and Williams, K. (2006) *Black teachers in London*. London: Greater London Authority.

Foreword
by Bell Ribeiro-Addy MP,
Labour Member of
Parliament for Streatham

In May 2021, Boris Johnson's government published its long-awaited Commission on Race and Ethnic Disparities (CRED). This was commissioned in response to the growing Black Lives Matter protests of the previous summer, which forced Britain to contemplate the racism that continues to shape the society we live in today. Just one year later, we were presented with a finished product: a report which set out in 258 pages how there was no such thing as institutional racism in our country. A far cry from the consciousness of the year before, its publication marked a turning point in the government's approach to racism. Gone is the polite, hand-wringing technocracy of unheeded inquiries piling up in dusty Whitehall archives; here is the denialism, trolling, and gaslighting reactionary politics.

In an age of overt government denial of institutional racism, anti-racist struggles take on renewed importance. In the inimitable words of Angela Davis, 'in a racist society, it is not enough to be non-racist; we must be anti-racist'. To understand how institutional racism continues to shape our country, we only have to look at our school system. The classroom mirrors the society we inhabit.

Living in a society where your own lived experiences are denied by those at the very top of the system can make it easy to feel like you're fighting a losing battle. Even as a Member of Parliament, I am not insulated from this. You can feel isolated, gaslit, unsure where to turn. When I rise to speak in the House of Commons, I can be confident in what I say and yet still feel imposter syndrome. Sometimes people are not listening to what you are saying as much as they are seeing who you are. As my colleague Diane Abbott MP once said, 'I could be reading the Yellow Pages and as far as they knew I would be saying, open the floodgates, let the migrants in'.

Like any Black child growing up in a majority white country, I remember how it felt to be treated differently in school, although I didn't necessarily have the language to express it at the time. Black children are up to twice as likely to face exclusion on average and up to six times more likely in some local authorities. Over the last decade, the total number of Black children living in poor households has more than doubled. More than half of Black children in the UK are now growing up in poverty. When a Black child goes to school, they are more likely to leave a household living in poverty, more likely to breathe polluted air on their route in, more likely to rely on free school meals at lunchtimes, more likely to face discrimination and racism, more likely to face violence, more likely to face exclusion, more likely to end up being criminalised, and more likely to end up in prison.

The backlash against the concept of institutional racism is partly a reaction to a growing consensus around the way racism is systematically reinforced across different institutions. It's about trying to undermine the idea that the people in charge of running the state might bear some responsibility for the impact of the policies carried out by the state. As reactionary voices try to construct a narrative where addressing the enduring inequalities faced by Black communities comes at the expense of the 'white working class', it's also about picking apart bonds of solidarity that might be created by mutual exploitation. Education is a more important battleground than ever.

For as long as diverse communities have made their home in the UK, people in positions of power have sought to exploit them and pit the working class against them. Like most people growing up in Britain over the past century, I never learned about the civil rights struggles in the UK. The concerted lack of education around the struggles that shaped our country is an attempt to occlude the fights that won the gains we enjoy today: from independence struggles in former colonies to the Bristol Bus Boycotts and the Battle of Lewisham. It is hard to overstate the psychological effects of these omissions. Not seeing yourself reflected in history has a damaging impact on your identity and sense of belonging.

The amnesia around our country's imperial past is inseparable from our neo-liberal present. As Kojo Koram persuasively argues in his recent book *Uncommon Wealth* (John Murray, 2022), the same policies that empowered corporate multinationals to gorge on the resources of newly independent colonies are now coming back to bite our own hollowed-out post-Brexit Brittania state. The establishment responds to the domestic scarcity created by its own political project by framing shoddy housing, falling wages and crumbling public services as a product of a fight for resources. It wants white working-class people to believe that Black and brown working-class people are benefitting at their expense, whilst presiding over an unprecedented transfer of wealth and power to the very richest in our society.

The idea that you can completely disaggregate class from race is absolutely central to the right-wing political project. In this sense, our struggle to decolonise schools is as much about class as it is race. It's no coincidence that other notable gaps in history lessons include the miners' strikes, the poll tax riots, and the accomplishments of trade unions. So often, efforts to write Black struggles back into history are also efforts to write working-class struggles back into history. If working-class kids learn about movements for change and how they persevered to challenge injustice, the real worry for the establishment is that these children might start recognising parallels with what is happening in our present.

Addressing racism in schools isn't holding back working-class pupils; not least because this is still not being done in any sort of systematic way. What is holding back working-class pupils is cuts to education budgets, academisation, excluding pupils, secure schools, and the funding crisis in special educational needs and disabilities provision. These policies disproportionately impact students from minority ethnic backgrounds but they are deeply harmful for working-class pupils across the board. Contra the reactionary nonsense, equality is not a zero-sum game. Our liberation is connected. By equipping all our children with an honest understanding of history and the realities of racism in the present, we can prepare them for life in a more equal country that truly respects and values diversity.

This is as true at the level of structure and form as at the level of content. By unpicking the racism woven through our education system, we can make it better for everyone, leaving teachers to be teachers, schools to be schools, and kids to be kids. This is no easy task. The acute pressures facing teachers right now, after a decade of school cuts and falling wages, are only compounded for Black teachers. In a system where discrimination remains rife and Black teachers are still under-represented – especially relative to pupil populations – Black teachers face higher levels of stress than their white colleagues, under-representation in senior management, lower levels of pay, and a persistent sense of being under-valued and under-supported. In a situation where the UK is heading for a retention and recruitment crisis in teaching, the failure to create a system that works for Black teachers is damaging for the entire school system, with Black teachers more likely to leave.

The first step towards dismantling oppressive structures is naming them. That's what is at stake when the government pushes back against efforts to describe the racism we experience on a daily basis. This handbook stands in a long tradition of Black self-organisation in education. It is a tool for teachers to create the truly just education system we all want to see.

Racism is something that is hurled down from the top of society, but change starts at the bottom. By building on the experiences and best practices of Black teachers working to create truly anti-racist education spaces, we can replicate these practices across our system. Too often, Black people are treated as the problem when, really, we're the solution.

1
Early Experiences in Education

Kemi – Why I do what I do

Black students who were exposed to Black teachers by third grade were 13% more likely to enrol in college. If kids had two Black teachers by third grade, Hart said, the likelihood of college enrollment jumped to 32%. (Ahébée, 2021, citing research by Gershenson et al., 2021)

She walked into my Year 1 class with a long, leather black mac coat (like the one Shaft used to wear), a short pixie cut, like Nia Long in the Fresh Prince of Bel Air; she wore glasses too just like I did. Her skin was the same colour as mine and she owned the room with her presence. Or maybe it was just me that noticed her the way I did. I was 5 years old at the time, but I remember a lot of details about her. The way she made an effort to pronounce people's names correctly when taking the register, how stern she looked, but she would smile from time to time. I remember the time I forgot my packed lunch at home the day I was going on a school trip and she took me to a bakery/sandwich shop and told me I could choose anything I wanted. My initial feeling of embarrassment disappeared. She had a son about my age too and when she brought him to school a couple of times, she treated him the same way she treated the rest of us in the class. No messing about.

I always tell people who ask, I never planned on becoming a teacher. In all honesty, I kind of just fell into it. It just happened. But looking back on my childhood, Ms M, although her time teaching me was very *very* short, she made such a mark in my childhood as the first Black teacher I ever had, that I still feel her impact to this very day. She planted a seed that other amazing teachers I met along the way, during my formal education years, watered, such as Ms S, Mr O, Ms A – they all watered it. I had amazing teachers who weren't Black as well, but still made a difference. But the Black teachers I personally encountered, felt familiar. The ones I met in secondary school were all African, so they felt even closer to home. I was far from the perfect student – I wasn't bad, I did OK in school – but Ms S, Ms A and Mr O all felt like the aunties and an uncle who wanted to see you win, who pushed you and challenged you even through the growing pains. Because of my relationship with all of these amazing teachers, I had more of an interest in the subjects they taught and I was engaged in their lessons.

I did notice that while I was in school, none of the Black teachers were in the senior leadership team (SLT). Middle leadership, maybe. Senior leadership, yeah right. It was an all-white ensemble. Secondary school was where I became more aware of my Blackness.

A group of Black kids hanging together at break or lunch time was seen as threatening, intimidating and a 'gang'. Teachers would always tell us to 'break up' as too many of us would hang about together in the same area of the playground. A group of white kids doing the same were just kids and they could continue as they were. The hairstyles we had in school were an issue as well. My friend who would dye her hair or get extensions that were a different colour to her natural hair, she was *always* told by the headteacher to take her braids out or dye her hair black; at the same time, there was another student who was white and would also dye her hair different colours, but she never got called to the headteacher's office or told to dye her hair black.

I never encountered a Black senior leader in school or even a Black lecturer when I went to university. The more aware I became of my Blackness as I got older, the more I realised it wasn't in the places and spaces I would've liked to see Black people occupy. Black people dominating a lot of sports and the arts was great, but how about in education and academia? We were there, but not visible enough. We were there, but the chances were limited or very few and far between.

We never celebrated Black History Month in school either. The one time we did anything close to Black history was when my history teacher made us watch the TV show *Roots* just before the summer holidays. Watching that only made me angry and resentful. I wasn't even aware of how brutal slavery was before then. My parents had told me of their racist experiences when they first moved to England and I knew my brothers had had similar experiences too, but slavery was never something that was spoken about. I never understood the aftermath and long-lasting effects, even until this day, and maybe it wasn't for me to understand back then as a child, but I was interested in learning and understanding more. I also never realised some of my experiences are what we now call microaggressions (that wasn't a word that was widely used when I was a student): the Black students that will always get told off by teachers even though white students were talking just as loud; the Black students who couldn't express themselves through their hair, but white students could; the Black boys who would be in class one day and then gone the next – I later found out they had been excluded from school. These were all things that just seemed to happen, but 'why' was not a question I asked and nor did I hear other people ask that question.

One year, I and another student took it upon ourselves to put on a Black History Month celebration. If the school weren't going to celebrate us, we would celebrate ourselves and we would do it loudly. We organised a great event that showcased people's talents through singing, spoken word, playing instruments, drama, and we had a fashion show that showed off our African outfits, complete with jollof rice and chicken (thanks to my mum). I needed the school to know that there was more to us than the negative stories in the media and the negative experiences a lot of students had in school.

After graduating from the University of Essex in 2013, my biggest fear was being a broke graduate. I didn't want to be another statistic. My parents had drummed education into my brothers and I so much until we completed our degrees, then it was like 'What next? What do I do with this piece of paper?' To be quite frank, school did not prepare me enough in terms of long-term goals and a career. I don't even remember talking to a careers advisor or counsellor about my future. I still wasn't completely sure what I wanted to do with my life moving forward. Until July 2013, education was my cushion, my safety net, a bubble that protected me to an extent from the real world, where I'd be forced to grow up and be an adult. I enjoyed working with young people and helping them, but I never saw myself as a teacher, let alone a science teacher. I thought I'd go into business and be an entrepreneur or something along those lines.

In September 2013, I started my role as a Learning Support Assistant (LSA) in a mainstream school in East London. The job wasn't strenuous for me at the time. I did what I had to do from 8.15am to 3.30pm and then I left. A couple of months into the role, another colleague and I were approached by a middle leader who said we were overqualified for our roles as LSAs (which we knew), but, for me at the time, that didn't matter. I was earning money, doing my job well and I enjoyed working and supporting my students. My colleague and I were then asked if we wanted to go into teaching. I had considered it, but I knew that if I was going to go down the education route again, I'd most likely be a PE teacher as I have a degree in Sport & Exercise Science. We were asked to teach English to students who were classed as 'English as an Additional Language' (EAL). How hard could it be teaching students basic punctuation, spelling and grammar? Most of them already knew how to read, so I thought I only had to fill in the gaps when it came to their writing. I underestimated how much work went into planning and delivering lessons. I did not enjoy the marking either, because half of the time I never understood what the students wrote. Their handwriting was illegible so Google Translate soon became my best friend when planning. I'd translate words from English into Lithuanian, Russian, Polish and other European languages. I spent hours on planning as we weren't given enough guidance or support; after all, we were not teachers. We were two LSAs, fresh out of university in the full-time working world, doing what we've been told to do. After a few weeks, I realised they placed students who were 'naughty' in our English classes. It was a dumping ground for negative behaviour, and who occupied the room most of the time? Black kids.

During my time as an LSA, I found myself saying 'yes' to a lot of things people would ask me to do, because I never wanted to be considered lazy, not a team player, difficult to work with, and so on. I never wanted to give anyone a reason to doubt my work ethic. I felt, and sometimes still feel, like I have to constantly prove myself.

When I trained as a science teacher in 2014 via the School Direct route, I was the only Black person in my cohort. I was surprised for one reason: this wasn't the 1950s, so where were the other Black people? Surely I couldn't be the only one. But I was. I never enjoyed teaching as a trainee, a newly qualified teacher and an NQT +1, but having Black colleagues definitely made a difference and they made sure I didn't quit.

The way I saw white middle and senior leaders speak to Black colleagues, in comparison to the way they spoke to white colleagues, sometimes made me sick. I will admit, I didn't always speak up. During my NQT year, I became a staff governor and it was made very apparent that a few members of the SLT were not happy: 13 white men, two white women and a Black woman sitting round a table, discussing the ins and outs of the school. I stood out like a sore thumb, just like during my training year. I didn't break a sweat and I didn't crumble when they asked me questions, but I could see their skin crawl from the simple fact that I was there and I enjoyed seeing the uncomfortable look on their faces. If my presence, as someone who was voted in by staff to represent them as a staff governor, made governors feel uncomfortable, that wasn't my problem.

I remember working in a school where the headteacher said 'because there are more Black kids coming to this school, white parents aren't sending their children here and that's having an impact on admissions and pupil intake'. My head had never turned so quickly; I think I gave myself whiplash. That's when I knew I had to talk up, speak my mind and stand up for what was right, even if it did put me in the line of fire. I may not have articulated myself in a way they would've liked, but I didn't care at that moment.

Becoming a staff governor made me realise I wanted to progress in my career; I wanted to be more than a teacher. I wanted to be in a position of influence when it came to decisions that concerned the students under my duty of care. I wanted to be a policy maker. I wanted to have more of a say and I wanted my voice to be heard, especially by those who may have thought I had nothing worth saying.

The stresses and politics of teaching have made me want to give up many times since 2013, but my students have always made me stay. No one gets into teaching for the money; there are many other sectors that would pay more and we all know teachers are overworked and underpaid. If you don't know, let's agree to disagree. Working in mainstream schools as well as a Pupil Referral Unit (PRU) has reaffirmed my love and passion of working with young people and ensuring they have what they need to succeed in school and beyond the classroom. I have progressed from class teacher to Careers Leader. I want students to know what their options are when they leave formal education. I want them to be exposed to careers and sectors they never even knew existed. I want students to encounter Black people who are in various roles and positions and make a difference. I want students to understand the importance of networking and making meaningful connections.

I also became the trips coordinator. I've worked with a lot of students who had never even left their local area. They had never been into central London, or eaten in a nice restaurant, or visited a university campus. Being a trips coordinator allowed me to take my students away from their local high street and see what else was out there for them to explore and discover.

I became a qualified SENCO in 2020. In 2017–2021, when I worked in a PRU, 90% of our students were Black. Black students never made 90% of the school population in the borough, so why were they always in my class? The exclusion rates for Black pupils was shocking in comparison to white students. Over the years, I've found that teachers lack patience and empathy when dealing with Black students in comparison to white ones. I've heard colleagues use words like 'scary' and 'intimidating' when describing Year 7 students who were less than 5 feet tall. I've had colleagues blame Black students for doing something wrong, because the student stood out due to their height, weight and skin colour (even if they don't want to admit it to themselves). I've had a number of students go under the radar for so long in the mainstream or be labelled because of their 'bad behaviour', rather than addressing the fact that they have a special educational need that has not been diagnosed or met by the school or local authority.

I didn't want to leave any child behind anymore, so I became a SENCO to ensure the students who were given negative labels got their needs met before they were put back into a mainstream environment.

References

Ahébée, S. (2021) 'They see me as a role model': Black teachers improve education outcomes for Black students [online], 19 February. https://whyy.org/segments/they-see-me-as-a-role-model-black-teachers-improve-education-outcomes-for-black-students (accessed 30 January 2024).

Gershenson, S., Hart, C., Hyman, J., Lindsay, C. and Papageorge, N. (2021) The long-run impacts of same-race teachers. NBER Working Paper Series no. 2524 [online]. www.nber.org/system/files/working_papers/w25254/w25254.pdf (accessed 30 January 2024).

Caren – 'How did you survive that?!' (G.I., 2010)

When Facebook first started, I was at university and the sum total of people's experience of me was my present-day presentation, circa 2005: Black girl, funny accent, loves reading, white girl name and the life and soul of any partaaaaay! I was definitely wearing 'white face' and doing a decent job of existing in white spaces. For most of my life, that's all I had ever known. I was born in Kenya and moved to the UK aged 5 with my family. Most of my childhood memories of Kenya became fragments of nostalgia that I would retreat to when things became tough in the north. From Newcastle to Edinburgh, I spent the next 15 years navigating a world with rules no one had taught me. Luckily, I wasn't alone, but survival was the name of the game. In most classrooms, I was the only Black face and in most schools, the majority of the other Black people there were related to me (I was the second of four children at home).

From our arrival, I understood the immigrant assignment: keep your head down and get on with it. And get on with it we did. I went from primary to secondary school knowing that I must always be the most non-threatening version of a Black person, lest the latent racist within my peers/teachers would be activated. I say this with no malice. Yes, I had some lovely teachers and plenty of friends at school, for which I am very thankful. Shout out to so many of the teachers at my Edinburgh secondary school who made me feel I could just be 'me'. However, I can't ignore years of being called my sister's name in every room I walked into (she's that other Black girl in the school, you see); or snide comments made by teachers and support staff that didn't believe in my abilities. The audacity of my Head of Year in one secondary school advising me to be a hairdresser, despite me acing every exam and test we sat. It wasn't until I went to university and found other people like me that I finally felt I could semi-retire my mask and literally be loud and unapologetically me.

Fast forward to the start of my teaching career and the uncovering of my childhood sports' team photos on Facebook, which caused my teacher friend 'G' to gasp in utter shock. She looked at me aghast and contemplated (through a series of musings and questions) what effect existing as a Black person in white spaces could have had on me? I believe it's best summed up by W.E.B. Dubois' term 'double consciousness' (Du Bois, 1903). At all times – although unbeknownst to childhood me – I had carried the burden of always looking at myself through the eyes of (white) society. Be it what I should bring in for lunch (it couldn't be too smelly or foreign sounding) or the pronunciation of my middle name Akoth (it had the pesky habit of popping up unexpectedly on reward certificates etc.) ... life up north was no bed of roses. I think I was lucky in that my parents and older sister absorbed most of the vitriol and I could vicariously learn lessons through the challenges and obstacles they faced. It left me woefully unprepared for life in a multicultural society, but an absolute expert in 'whitespeak' (Law and Corrigan, 2018).

How did all of this shape my educational journey? I learned that it was important to ask for things in modal verbs – 'please may/could I?' rather than being a 'typical Black girl'. I learned it was important to always get the top grades. Middle or bottom wasn't an option. I learned that I had to have 100% attendance and excel in every extra-curricular activity. Most importantly, I learned that my parents should *never ever* be called for bad behaviour. I couldn't even bring myself to tell them when I got my first detention in Year 8. Even as a young girl in preinternet days, I knew exactly what stereotypes teachers were waiting for me to bust out and my parents had warned us in no uncertain terms – we were never to fall into those traps. I crafted myself into the perfect student and was always on the tip of each teacher's tongue for recommendations and commendations. At the time, it seemed very enjoyable and life felt easy, but ... underneath the surface, trouble was brewing.

Needless to say, my childhood educational experiences were filled with all the joys and tribulations that most young people in the '90s in northern England can remember: Boyzone, Take That, trackies and a proximity to 'chav' culture. My parents did their best to keep us (myself and my three siblings) away from all of that by enrolling us in countless extra-curricular activities which filled our time and minds. We also served in church (music, altar, etc.) and that pretty much filled our days. When we moved to Edinburgh, I was in my teens and my family were ready for a fresh start. Academically, things remained exactly the same for me, but as a family, we talked a lot more about the challenges of growing up as an African teenager in the west. Our conversations became more frank and the microaggressions that we faced at school, or in our extra-curricular activities, were explored and dissected at home. The bond I had with my siblings at the time was unbreakable. It was akin to those going through war together, knowing that, at some point, there would be a ray of light.

What was my ray of light? I travelled to Botswana as part of a charity project when I was 17. Despite multiple trips to Kenya with my family throughout my childhood, this was the first time I felt Black in Africa. Why was that? I was, once again, the only Black person in a white space. It had not occurred to my teenage mind when I was signing up and fundraising to secure my spot on the trip, that every other participant would be white (or white other) and that *everyone* in Botswana would be Black. This came to a head when we started the group projects. Our task was to paint a primary school. Groundbreaking? No. Life-changing? No. The right step to eradicating poverty in that area? Absolutely not. White saviour leaning? 100% yes.

It dawned on me in a series of steps and missteps that I was one of 'them' – the locals – and not necessarily one of the group of charity do-gooders. After that trip, I have refused to buy a fairtrade banana or engage in any 'poverty-eradicating' international charity work, as anyone who travels to a so-called 'third world' country can tell you – it's all window dressing. Did we Make Poverty History in 2005? Or in any year since then? No. Will we? Not unless the powers that be truly want a fair, just and equal society. But, I digress.

After that moment of awakening, several things started to happen. It was like a fire had been lit inside me. I had to do my part to change society! Much to my parents' chagrin, I boldly declared that I would not be going straight to university after sixth form, and I applied for a gap year when making my applications to university. I started to read outside of the reading lists provided by educational establishments and I made plans to travel to America – the mecca of Black people to my teenage mind. I worked at a summer camp and then went to live in New York with some of the camp staff after the season ended. These decisions all had the impact of opening my mind even more to a world I had never envisioned.

I decided I was going to work in education and share this growing knowledge with those who needed it. My zeal was uncontainable and totally unrealistic! This was the first moment I started to think I may choose teaching as a career. I dabbled with the thought of becoming an educational psychologist, but after shadowing one, I could see they wouldn't have much day-to-day impact with young people. I volunteered for as many charities as I could in Edinburgh and later at university, so that I could understand what barriers to educational success young people faced. I was on the student union at university in York and in countless societies. I certainly wasn't going to waste any opportunities! Then came Cambridge and it was all I had dreamed it would be. I found my spirit equivalents and we partied endlessly whilst writing essays when we got home from clubbing. The definition of burning the midnight oil was our lives. Despite so many challenges during my PGCE (more on this later in the book), I completed the course, became a teacher and started at an academy serving the students of Tottenham. I was here! I was at the destination! Little did I know there was much, much, much more to come...

I progressed rapidly in the school, leaping from one promotion to the next, very much down to my then ability to work hard, play hard: last to leave my classroom/desk and last one to leave the pub. I made some absolute legends of friends as a teacher at the school and two are now godmothers to my daughter. From Nando's, to Starbucks, to the pub next door – the social scene was lit and fuelled by many a dram. Thank heavens I had grown up in Newcastle and Edinburgh; no one could outparty me! There was so much learning and growth in that first school and I look back on it fondly. The (white, male) headteacher believed and invested in me, supporting me to go back to Cambridge and do a Master's in School Leadership, sending me on lots of courses and rounding off so many of my rough edges. It was in one of our free-period chats that he disclosed to me he had actually grown up in Africa and it dawned on me that he probably understood more about the 'good immigrant mindset' (Common Future, 2021) than most.

My next stop was an outstanding secondary school, still serving the students of Tottenham. I absolutely loved that school and the headteacher still ranks as the best head I've ever encountered. His belief in me was evident from our first phone conversation, and his gentle, inspiring, patient leadership, as well as his commitment to the family ethos of the school, is one I hope to emulate one day, if I'm resilient enough to make it to headship. His genuine love for the community and ability to bring out the best in even the toughest of cookies (adult or child) was incredibly inspiring. His compassion for the challenges many of 'us' face in our careers, was unmatched. Between him and his number two (both male – one northern white and the other Black Nigerian), you felt safe as a teacher and educator. Always supported. I'm sure the students and families we served felt the same. Unfortunately, the pace of the school was just too slow for me and I worried I would never make it up the ladder if I stayed in one place for too long. What a mistake! I should have let the grass grow under my feet, as there truly was/is no school like this one.

I went on to work at a few other schools, one a private school which showed me that the only difference between the state and private sector is the expectations of the adults. Teenagers in private schools also exhibit the full range of at-risk behaviours we see in the state sector and yet their parents and teachers demonstrate an unflinching, concerted and consistent effort to get them the top grades. Students who would struggle to get a pass (grade C in old money) in state school, were leaving with Bs and As. I was the same teacher, but the system was set up for them to succeed. No parent ever missed parents' evening, or dodged a call from the school. No uniform item was missing and certainly no trainers or hoodies were worn to school. I say this not to denigrate the state system (it's where I currently still teach), but to say that basic standards and expectations go a long way in setting the mindset of a pupil. If you know that everyone around you wants the best for you, believes in you and won't stop pushing until you become your best self, you will probably rise to the challenge. Especially if all of these adults are singing from the same hymn sheet.

One notable point on my journey that I can't avoid mentioning, is the discovery of the school bully. This could be a headteacher, a senior leader, a receptionist, or even your colleague next door. Sadly, the existence of bullies in playgrounds around the world means that the same characters exist in adulthood, only the playgrounds translate into board rooms and staffrooms. Discovering that 'work hard, play hard' wasn't enough to get me through in every setting was a shock to my system. I was unlucky enough to meet a leader – let's call him The Hidebehind for now – who, despite proclaiming to be a 'man of the people', turned out to be a soul-destroying ghoul. He was responsible for crushing more careers and dreams than any TV-based reality show. I also met the modern-day version of Ms Trunchbull and she did not disappoint. With vicious text messages, emails, whispered comments and endless eye-rolls, she orchestrated the demise of many teachers' careers. The worst one was Uncle Tom. If you know, you know.

Despite facing these challenges, I and countless other Black teachers have persevered, risen up and continued to strive towards the educational outcome we all seek: students like us (be it Black, Black other, or marginalised by any other name) achieving the grades they need, in order to open the doors that are often closed to them. This book is for you. I see you, I hear you and I implore you – don't give up. We are the change we seek.

References

Common Future (2021) *The power of the immigrant mindset* [online], 22 September. https://medium.com/commonfuture/the-power-of-the-immigrant-mindset-8a0f182f0916 (accessed 6 March 2024).

Du Bois, W.E.B. (1903) *The souls of Black folk: Essays and sketches*. Chicago, IL: A.C. McClurg & Co.

Law, M. and Corrigan, L.M. (2018) On white-speak and gatekeeping: Or, what good are the Greeks? *Communication and Critical/Cultural Studies*, 15(4), 326–330.

Big question

What will the education sector look like in years to come, for example, for children who are born today? How do we ensure that there is representation at all levels so they can see themselves in those who teach them?

2
Why We Need More Black Teachers

Caren

The answer to this 'why' is simple and yet profound: because students of colour, and particularly Black students, need to be seen, heard and understood in order to feel safe and to thrive in what they inherently see as a wider societal system set up for them to fail. From housing, to local issues, to education and their parents' daily lived experiences, many students of colour often learn to mistrust the system from a young age due to well-documented racial disparities (Gillborn et al., 2021).

These (and all) students need their potential to be nurtured and affirmed. They need to be taught from a starting position of success and empathy, rather than from a belief that something is 'wrong' with them, which needs remedying. Usually, and unfortunately, in the form of a white saviour. What is a white saviour, you ask? Think of films such as *The Blind Side* and *The Help* and the picture becomes clear. A well-meaning and often naïve protagonist sets forth in their 'quest' to 'fix' a societal issue, often confronting their own underlying prejudice, struggling to be understood and yet, by some miracle, still 'saving the world' or the microcosm their journey represents. This bildungsroman story has a worrying angle, with many teacher training organisations capitalising on a story that becomes about the protagonist (and their ego) and no longer about the societal issue they sought to 'fix'.

Herein lies the rub: how many WASP-esque teachers are parachuted into struggling schools to do their two years of service to society, often leaving with the same perspectives they came in with (regarding the communities they are serving) and none the wiser about how to actually address the underlying issues? How many students are excluded because of these mindsets? How many students end up joining a prison pipeline because, instead of compassion, understanding, a listening ear and patience, they were met with an unrelenting system that did not stop to take into account that this morning the student had to get all of their siblings ready, drop them off at school, and had no chance to do their homework last night, as there was no space or quiet time ... and is now starving as they wait for their free school meal lunch credit to kick in, so they can have breakfast at lunchtime?

I am by no means making excuses for the said student, or allowing their parents to scapegoat 'the education system'. However, over two decades since the Macpherson report revealed to us that 'institutional racism' was at the centre of British society (Criminal Justice Alliance, 2020), we still needed David Lammy's 2017 review to confirm that the prejudice Black and minority ethnic children face is a 'social timebomb' (Lammy, 2017), which the Covid-19 pandemic undeniably revealed with 'the unequal impact of Covid-19 on BAME communities [stemming from] a number of factors ranging from social and economic inequalities, racism, discrimination and stigma [and] occupational risk' (BBC, 2020; Public Health England, 2020). Can these issues truly be unrelated? According to the Criminal Justice Alliance (2020), 'systemic and institutional racism still persists within policing and the wider criminal justice system'. Is it any wonder that in the classroom and across the education system 'black pupils in some areas of England were more than three times more likely to be excluded from school than their peers in 2017–18' (Gibbon, 2020)?

How does that look on a Monday morning when a teacher is stressed and irritable? How does it look on a Friday afternoon when said student has 'had enough' for that week? How does it look when after a six-period day, that student kisses their teeth at you? These are the everyday scenarios where mindset, perspective and compassion can have life-altering outcomes. Instead of that student being sent to the 'seclusion' room or to their Head of Year, or being picked up by the senior leadership team for an after-school detention (and then acting out because their siblings will be waiting in the cold), the student may be given a time-out, have a respectful 1-to-1, or even come back at the end of the day for a five-minute chat where the teacher asks 'what's going on?'. I have seen 6-foot bad-men of the school almost reduced to tears when I look in their eyes and actually ask them 'what's going on and how can I help?'. Would I care so much if I wasn't Black? Maybe. Maybe not. But when I look out at those brown and Black faces, I see my brother, nephews, uncles and, most importantly, my father. Would I be who and where I am today if my father had been over-sanctioned and over-policed? Would he have made it to doctoral-level studies if he had not had his learning power nurtured and affirmed? My father grew up believing he could be anything and do anything in colonial East Africa. Surely, in London in 2024 we can do even better?

To be able to nurture this feeling in teachers, we as educators need to feel supported too. That is why networks are of the utmost importance. The advice I give to all trainee teachers is to get out of the classroom and network. Get to know other teachers, their approaches and how other schools do things. Visit other establishments and challenge your way of thinking. There are many ways to 'skin a cat' and the cat we need to skin is discriminatory practices when teaching and sanctioning brown and Black children. We need to support each other as educators with so much: managing upwards and downwards, liaising with difficult colleagues, managing the daily microaggressions (they will come…trust me) and just reaffirming our purpose(s). We need to remind ourselves that the mountain is not going to be climbed alone. As one African proverb says: 'If you want to go fast, go alone; but if you want to go far, go together'.

References

BBC (2020) *Coronavirus: Racism 'could play a part in BAME Covid deaths'*. BBC News, 13 June. www.bbc.co.uk/news/health-53035054.

Criminal Justice Alliance (2020) Twenty one years after Macpherson Report, systemic racism in policing continues, 10 July. www.criminaljusticealliance.org/blog/twenty-one-years-after-macpherson-report-systemic-racism-in-policing-continues.

Gibbon, A. (2020) Exclusion rates higher for some BAME pupils. *TES* [online], 30 July. www.tes.com/news/school-exclusion-rates-higher-some-bame-pupils-data-shows.

Gillborn, D., Bhopal, K., Crawford, C.E., Demack, S., Gholami, R., Kitching, K., Kiwan, D. and Warmington, P. (2021) Evidence for the commission on race and ethnic disparities. Working paper, University of Birmingham. http://epapers.bham.ac.uk/3389 (accessed 7 March 2024).

Lammy, D. (2017) The racial bias in our justice system is creating a social timebomb. *The Guardian*, 8 September. www.theguardian.com/commentisfree/2017/sep/08/david-lammy-review-bame-children-face-prejudice-flawed-criminal-justice-system.

Public Health England (2020) *Beyond the data: Understanding the impact of COVID-19 on BAME groups*. https://assets.publishing.service.gov.uk/government/uploads/system/uploads/attachment_data/file/892376/COVID_stakeholder_engagement_synthesis_beyond_the_data.pdf

Kemi

According to the government's teacher workforce census (DfE, 2023), in 2021, Black teachers (African, Caribbean and other) made up 2.5% of the teacher workforce in England. In 2024, we are still dealing with the issue of a lack of Black teachers and senior leaders in the education sector. Research by NFER published in January 2024 showed, despite Black teachers being overrepresented during the application stage of teacher training, we are underrepresented in the profession and low acceptance rates compared to white counterparts is a contributing factor.

It is important to take into account that this data does not include independent schools, sixth form colleges and other further educational establishments. That is a total of approximately 11,400 teachers in England, compared to 421,000 white teachers. This is not far off the number of Black people in England. According to the 2011 census, Black people make up 3.3% of the population in England and Wales. Which means that out of 56.1 million people in England and Wales, there was a total of 1.9 million Black people.

From 2001 to 2011, the number of Black Africans in England and Wales doubled. The number of Black Caribbeans has remained the same, which is 1.1%, and the number of Black other has increased by 0.3%.

So, what does this all mean for education? Although the percentage of Black teachers in education is not that far off the percentage of Black people in England and Wales, it is important to take into account that most Black teachers work in inner-London, state-funded schools, and that there is a higher population of Black students in this area. There is a greater need for representation in these schools as most Black students in inner London are from deprived areas.

Out of 11,400 teachers, 3,200 are Black men in comparison to over 8,200 Black women. This is a further lack of representation for our Black boys/young men, which cannot be ignored. I mean, it is no surprise that there are more women teachers than men. However, there are more men in senior leadership levels compared to women. This isn't applicable to our Black men and women though, as you hardly see us in a headship position, and, quite frankly, it's poor. These numbers continue to decrease as teachers progress into leadership positions, further supporting the fact that there is a lack of representation in education. If you thought compulsory education was bad, it gets even worse as we move into higher education. According to the Higher Education Statistics Agency (HESA, 2024), less than 1% of the professors in UK universities are Black.

This is the reason why organisations like the Black Teachers Network (BTN), BAMEd, DiverseEd, Black Teachers Connect and others are important and exist. Although different, they are also similar in the sense that they want all levels of the education sector to be reflective of multicultural Britain today and moving forward. These organisations and many others pushing for diversity, equality, inclusion and equity are transforming the face of education, not only for teachers, but also for the next generation: our children and their future.

I've always valued education and held it in high regard. Coming from a working-class Nigerian family, my parents drummed the value of education into my brothers and I from a very young age. As a child, it was sometimes annoying. Now as an adult and a teacher myself, I find that those same values follow me into the classroom and I drum them into my children (my students). I am beyond grateful for the sacrifices my parents made to be where they are now and to give my brothers and I the best start to life. As a child, whenever I used to correct my mum's grammar, she'd remind me, 'My parents had to pay for my English, you got yours for free'. Where students have the privilege of being educated for free in the UK, I want them to be the absolute best that they can be in my classroom and beyond, especially the Black boys and girls who see me as a reflection of themselves. I know you've just read a whole lot of stats and figures when it comes to Black teachers in education and trust me, it's not just about numbers. We want those with a passion for young people in the profession. We want to retain those who are already in the profession by ensuring they feel valued and are aware of opportunities to progress into leadership, if they choose to do so. We want both teaching and non-teaching staff to know we value what they bring to the table inside and outside of the classroom. We are raising aspirations of the next generation and ourselves. We know and believe that students need to see representation of themselves in every sector and every position. What and who we represent are real in and out of the classroom; we are not just role models, acting on a daily basis. This isn't an acting gig; this is our reality.

References

Department for Education (DfE) (2023) *School teacher workforce*. [online] www. ethnicity-facts-figures.service.gov.uk/workforce-and-business/workforce-diversity/school-teacher-workforce/latest.

Higher Education Statistics Agency (HESA) (2024) Higher Education Staff Statistics: UK 2022/23, 16 January [online]. www.hesa.ac.uk/news/16-01-2024/higher-education-staff-statistics-uk-202223 (accessed 30 January 2024).

National Foundation for Educational Research (NFER) (2024) *Ethnic diversity in the teaching workforce: Evidence review*. www.nfer.ac.uk/media/py4nu3eq/ethnic_diversity_in_the_teaching_workforce_embargoed.pdf (accessed 6 March 2024).

Big question

What do diversity and representation look like in your school? Are they a tick-box exercise or are they embedded in the fabric of the school ethos and culture?

3

Varied Routes into Teaching

Kemi

There are varied routes into teaching, just like there are different ways of teaching. It isn't a 'one size fits all kind of approach'. It is important that you do your research and due diligence to find what works for you; how you learn and what fits with your current lifestyle and financial commitments and so on.

My original plan wasn't to become a teacher, but when I did decide to teach as a career, the only route I personally knew was going back to university and completing my Post Graduate Certificate in Education (PGCE). I applied to St Mary's and Greenwich University, hoping that one of them would accept me. To be honest with you, my anxiety was through the roof, as I wasn't particularly keen on going back to university and spending another academic year feeling like I wasn't ready or good enough, and continuously second-guessing myself. I had spent three years of my life doing that during my undergraduate degree.

I went to my interviews for both universities and, of course, I was the only Black person in the room, but I was so prepared or as prepared as I could be. I mean, I had to be because I had to leave my house at 5am to get there for 8am and that was a long journey; there was absolutely no way I messed up that interview. I genuinely believed I had aced my interview at St Mary's. I heard back from them a few days later that I was unsuccessful, which meant all I had left was Greenwich and they had to take me; there was no other choice, or so I thought.

I attended my Greenwich interview more prepared than my interview at St Mary's. This had to go in my favour. I took part in the group activities and the written assessment I had to complete, and I felt good about both. There was nothing more I could do. Then it was time for my 1:1 interview with one of the tutors/lecturers. I was prepared to tell them about my passion for young people, my experience thus far and the value of education that my parents had instilled in me, how I was ready to spark the minds of young people and teach science in a fun and engaging way to ensure their love of learning continued throughout their educational journey. But the question I was asked threw me off: '*What happens when you eat a cheese sandwich?*' As a biology specialist, I knew the answer, but my mind went blank, so to the interviewer I clearly did not know the answer. I answered it anyway, regurgitating all the information I knew about the digestive system. I walked away from that interview knowing for sure that Greenwich would not accept me.

The next day at work, the headteacher stopped me in the corridor and asked how my interview went; I told her. She went on to say that she didn't want the school to lose out on fresh young talent and passionate people who know the school and the students well, and proposed the idea of me training to be a teacher whilst getting paid to teach. I had no idea that was even an option. A few days later, I received a conditional offer from the University of Greenwich. Now I had options. Once I knew my place was secure on the school's direct teacher training programme through e-Qualitas, I declined the offer from Greenwich. From day one, I was thrust into the classroom; making seating plans and markbooks, planning lessons, teaching theory and practicals, managing behaviour, working collaboratively with my TAs (which was weird because I was just a TA) and attending department meetings. It was full on from the get go and balancing my assignments and off-site teacher training days with working full time was overwhelming. Alongside health issues at the time and then losing 16 weeks' worth of my teacher training evidence for my portfolio and a 10,000-word essay on personalised learning; I was ready to quit. In fact, I wrote my resignation letter and showed it to my line manager. She took the letter and said she wouldn't accept it. She told me to keep pushing through and that the whole department would help get back everything I had lost as well as give me time off teaching to focus on rewriting my essay. I cried. All I needed to do was ask for help, but I didn't because I didn't want to look incompetent. During my training year, my line manager was the real MVP (most valuable player) who ensured that I didn't quit. She clearly saw something in me that I didn't.

The on-the-job training was intense and School Direct is no joke, even though I never had a 25-hour teaching timetable, I had 18. Some may say, it's not a lot, but for me it was. However, in hindsight, it was the best decision I could've made. Nothing could beat the invaluable first-hand experience of teaching I got from day one; those away learning days gave me a break from the classroom, but also provided practical strategies and techniques that I would later implement in my lessons. There was also the support of my line manager, knowing the school and the students so well and being able to earn money at the same time, because I had a fear of being a broke graduate and not being able to take care of myself.

The skills, knowledge and understanding I gained through the School Direct programme was second to none for me. It made me more resilient and gave me even more respect for teachers. That first year as a trainee showed me the many hats that teachers wear on a daily basis. Inevitably, we are parents to children that are not biologically ours, even before some of us really become parents ourselves.

Caren

My route into teaching was very traditional and inspired by my teenage experiences of volunteering. At first, the goal was to become an educational psychologist, so the focus was on attaining the Graduate Basis for Registration from a prestigious establishment. I spent many an hour poring over prospectuses and websites, deciding which university to apply to, to study psychology. The arrogance of youth told me that it didn't matter where I applied, I was sure to get in. I was top of my class in all of my Highers (A-Level) subjects and had just won the Psychology Award in my borough for my S5 (Y12) results. I was humbly knocked back by UCL and Oxford, but luckily got into my other choices. York won the day as they gave me an unconditional offer and I got to spend S6 exploring Edinburgh's nightlife with my sixth form friends and doing very little studying!

After graduation, I was off to America to see what all the fuss was about! It didn't disappoint. I literally had the *best* summer of my life as a teenager. No parents, few rules and an adult lifestyle? Yes, please! I learned more about myself in that summer than I had in 18 years in the UK. I also saw first hand how ingrained racism and ignorance are in the everyday American psyche. I was asked on an almost daily basis for the first cycle if I was 'really from the UK'. I felt tempted to carry a copy of my passport, but instead I just smiled and laughed along, feeling incredibly uncomfortable. My rescue came in the form of a fellow Black person who arrived to teach alongside us a few weeks in. I stuck to them like glue and the questions stopped.

Upon my return to the UK, I volunteered with Positive Help and The Scouts in Edinburgh, alongside working and travelling to see friends who were also on gap years abroad. Suffice to say, these were some wonderful months.

When autumn rolled around, I packed up my belongings and my parents drove me down to York. The first weekend was awful as they had got my accommodation wrong and I just wanted to go home. I dug deep and took myself off to the Freshers' Fair and Ball, where within 24 hours I had connected with my sister from another mister. It's not an understatement to say that as two Black African girls who had grown up outside London, we stuck out like sore thumbs! In many ways, this was both a blessing and a curse. We stuck together like two peas in a pod and even applied to the same postgraduate course to become teachers together. During our time at university, we were on the same committees for the ACS, Student Union and various other social clubs. We even started a mentoring scheme with local schools to partner with university students of colour.

Once I was at Cambridge, I took 'work hard, play hard' to another level, as mentioned before. I had some amazing times and my first school placement with my mentor was fantastic. Going into my second placement, I felt as though I had found my calling. That was when I met Cruella de Vil: living, breathing and definitely not pleased to see a Black trainee teacher in *her* classroom. I don't know if she had read the trainee form and only seen my first name? She seemed perpetually shocked that I could construct a sentence or that I even knew what a pronoun was. The level of scrutiny she put me through was unbelievable, but I had the support of my university mentor, and glowing reports from my first placement in the bank meant that her stabs in the dark landed nowhere. It was my first taste of someone in power disliking me 'on sight' and it was actually very scary to think that with the stroke of her pen, she could have ended my teaching career right there and then.

Still reeling from this placement, I was determined to work in London, but I wasn't sure if I could be bothered with the two years of teaching before I could become an Ed. Psych. A friend told me about this fantastic agency that was guaranteed to get you a good job and into a decent school. I was on the precipice of quitting as a teacher and thought 'why not?'. Within weeks of moving to London with some friends from university, we were up to our usual partying and social antics. I kept my head down and focused on passing my NQT year. The students were energetic, to say the least, and I seemed to have been given all the 'behaviour' classes … but I didn't quit. Those brown and Black faces inspired me daily and some of my fellow trainees were willing to join me on Saturday afternoons when we wanted to come in to school to mark and plan. We made friends with the Deputy Head who lived locally and he would open the school for us whenever we asked.

By Christmas, my headteacher was actually saying hello to me and my fellow trainees were urging me to try out the pub next door. The only way I can explain it was one day it was just 'Miss Onanda, English NQT' and the next day it was 'heyyyyy Caren'. I embraced the moment and got to know all these cool kids next door. They just happened to be the head of sixth form, various SLT and middle leaders. In all seriousness, allowing them to see the 'real me' and vice versa actually resulted in some of the best years of my teaching career. Race aside, we had so many good times and I only had to tell them off once or twice when it came to Black politics. Case in point: 'you can't be Catholic, Caren. I thought all Black people went to Pentecostal churches'. Yes, that really happened.

My rise through the ranks at that particular school was only stalled by the arrival of Ms Trunchbull. I was young and didn't have the energy for a re-run of the 'prove yourself' game; so, four years in and with consistently great exam results, I felt I could find another home in teaching. I had been having so much fun I had abandoned my plans to become an ed. psych and was firmly focused on staying in teaching for the long haul.

One weekend during Ms Trunchbull's reign, I was visiting a friend in Golders Green and the next week I found myself being interviewed for a role in her brother's school. I got the job and cheekily went for another interview at another school, just to let Trunchbull know that I could get a job anywhere. As I left my NQT home, I was filled with fear and anxiety, but also excitement. As previously mentioned, I had some amazing experiences with some fantastic headteachers and leaders. But, I can't fail to mention that two experiences in particular made me rethink my commitment to teaching. It's only with 20/20 hindsight that I can call these experiences out for what they were: bullying. I've seen so many teachers (and even experienced shades of it myself in recent years) leave the profession because someone marked their card. It's vital that we look out for each other and be our 'brother's keeper'. If you spot a teacher with a 'funny' accent struggling, or a senior/middle leader constantly poking holes in a member of staff, offer the said teacher support. You might be the first friendly face they have seen that day, week or term. Sit with them, help them plan, send them lessons and resources, and don't turn your back. I was incredibly lucky I had built my networks early on at university and in my teaching career, as well as in my personal life, that I was never short of a reference or referral. As highlighted in the 2018 NEU report on the impact of racism on teachers from ethnic minorities, Black teachers strongly felt that they were 'isolated and lacking in management support with regards to incidences of racism and career progression' (Haque and Elliott, 2018). Truer words were never spoken. The real danger facing amazing Black teachers is not classroom behaviour or difficult parents; but navigating the murky waters of personality politics. If you choose to engage, we salute you! This game is not for the faint-hearted. Seek help and support at every turn. I did and it saved me.

Fast forward to the present day and I count every single one of those challenges as a blessing. I have helped, and hope to continue to help, any teacher I see struggling, regardless of race. I hope that as I move through senior leadership, I won't become blind to microaggressions or forget to check in with that member of staff logging countless behaviour points. I hope that I will have the confidence to 'stick up for them' publicly and, most importantly, to show compassion and understanding as they develop in their careers.

Reference

Haque, Z. and Elliott, S. (2018) *Visible and invisible barriers: The impact of racism on BME teachers.* London: National Union of Teachers. https://neu.org.uk/sites/default/files/2023-02/Barriers%20Report.pdf (accessed 6 March 2024).

Bianca Williams – My PGCE journey

Bianca is an associate assistant headteacher with a specialism in teaching A-Level Psychology. She is now in her tenth year of teaching and currently teaches in a mixed comprehensive secondary school situated in inner London.

The application process

The start of my teaching journey began in 2012. While in the second year of my psychology degree studies, I was eager to start preparing for the next chapter of my life post-university and began to explore different career options. I had always had a strong interest in studying psychology and had also thoroughly enjoyed my experience as a student mentor; a role that I obtained shortly after completing my second-year university exams. This role had been advertised through my university as part of the outreach programme that they offered to local secondary schools. Through participating in this programme, I was able to gain first-hand experience of working with young people; particularly those who were at risk of being excluded and therefore needed support with their behaviour management, as well as for their aspirations to be raised. Witnessing the positive impact that such programmes had on the lives of young people, led me to seek a profession that afforded me the opportunity to continue positively influencing the lives of young people. These experiences combined, proved to be the catalyst for my pursuit to enter the teaching profession.

At the time of applying for my Postgraduate Certificate in Education (PGCE), the Graduate Teacher Training Registry (GTTR) was the admissions service that applicants were encouraged to use and this platform was operated by UCAS. As most PGCE training programmes begin in September, my application process began one year prior to the expected start date of my course. Similar to UCAS, a reference was needed prior to paying for and sending the application. You were only able to make one application at a time, and these operated on a first-come, first-served basis. This was a key difference that I noticed in comparison to undergraduate course applications made through UCAS, and it therefore highlighted the importance of researching and carefully shortlisting universities in advance of applications. Social Science PGCE courses were not that popular at the time of my application and, as a result, very few universities offered these niche courses – competition was therefore extremely high and preparation was vital.

Shortly after applying to my first-choice university, I was invited for an interview and had been sent a document which detailed what to expect on the day. The interview day involved several sessions which included: a group activity involving other interviewees, a brief meeting with the professors to discuss current affairs that related specifically to education, a numeracy and literacy assessment, as well as a micro-lesson on a topic of our choosing. The day concluded with an individual interview. As nerve-wracking as the day was, I enjoyed the process as the tasks were engaging and the advanced information given was accurate and provided the opportunity to prepare well. Less than five days later, I received the much-anticipated news that my place had been confirmed, subject to meeting the required conditions which included the successful completion of the numeracy and literacy skills tests (within six weeks of accepting the conditional offer), a minimum 2:2-degree qualification, a health check, a DBS certificate, two weeks of work experience within an educational setting, and the completion of school orientation visit reports.

The skills test component of the application process I found to be most challenging due to the amount of time needed to prepare for these tests. I had also been in the process of finalising my third-year dissertation and preparing for my final examinations, so for this reason the timing wasn't the best, particularly with the added stress of having a six-week deadline to complete them! Thankfully, new reforms are now under discussion, which suggest that the skills test components may be removed from the application process in the near future – watch this space!

And we're in!

The PGCE course started within the first week of September and week one was action-packed with university tours, group presentations and lots of theory.

By the second week of university, we had completed our first micro-teach in front of our peers, and by the third week, we were straight into our first placement school. The programme ran for 36 weeks, and 24 of those weeks were spent in two different school/college placements. Time had also been embedded within the programme to return back to the university campus for theory lessons, and to touch base with our peers and professors. Each time we returned to the campus, it was interesting to hear of the stark differences between our placement experiences, and it really showed me the huge difference that having a supportive mentor and placement setting can have on your outlook on teaching. While I had been lucky to have extremely supportive and nurturing mentors, unfortunately not everyone had this experience and by Christmas, a few had chosen to withdraw from the programme in its entirety. With each month that passed, the challenges that came with the PGCE course intensified and we went from having the stress of only planning lesson starters to now planning full lessons and juggling the completion of our ever-growing assignments. Those on the course became each other's supportive network system and before we knew it, we had made it out onto the other side of our assignments and were graduating the following year with QTS and PGCE degree certificates in hand.

Teacher training courses are no 'walk in the park'. There will be times when you will have an 'I give up' moment. When this happens, always go back to your 'why' and your reasons for choosing to embark on the teaching journey. Chances are this will be enough to encourage you to keep pushing on!

PGCE top tips

- Get a study group/support system going amongst your fellow PGCE peers and provide a space where you can share good practice and pool resources together.
- The PGCE course that I chose offered 20 Level 7 credits at Master's level, which I was then able to use towards my Master's degree years later. This hugely helped to lower costs and to reduce the number of modules that I needed to complete. I would therefore highly recommend for anyone who wishes to study for their Master's at a later stage, to explore this route.
- Remember that everyone's PGCE experience will be unique, as this reflects the unique culture of each educational setting. If you are extremely unhappy with your placement setting, remember that your university subject mentors and professors are there to help you and would be happy to make adjustments and accommodate where they are able to!

- Take advantage of recruitment fairs and mock interview days by participating in them. There is a strong chance that the schools who volunteer to support on those days are keen to recruit!
- Don't be afraid to make mistakes. Be open and receptive to feedback, as this is where growth occurs!
- With teaching, there is never a dull day, and each day will be different from the last. Take the time to get to know your pupils, and build the classroom environment that works for you. This will help to make each day a little bit easier and is an excellent behaviour management tool!

Seyi Noibi – The whirlwind of PGCE and beyond

Seyi 'Ezekiel' Noibi (often nicknamed 'Zeeks') has been in the world of education since 2013, working in a variety of different roles from Deputy Head of Year, Head of Department to now Head of Faculty. Since then, the world of education has undergone turbulence in many ways but one thing that remains consistent is his passion and determination to inspire the next generation, whether they be younger or older, to realise their potential and, most importantly, effect change.

The Postgraduate Certificate in Education (PGCE), for me, was what I considered to be my passport elsewhere. To clarify, my intent was to teach abroad and I had discussed this with leaders at the secondary school I attended as a student and came back to in order to amass experience as a teaching assistant (TA) before I formally decided whether teaching, indeed, was the vocation for me.

One thing I cannot stress enough is arming yourself with the prerequisite 'battle experience' of being in the classroom, engaging with the students and learning about how schools function, because the world I knew as a student only loosely compared to the world I encountered when embarking on my journey to become an educator. I can say this retrospectively now but because the PGCE experience offers such a hybrid approach of being a student-voyeur, a fledgling classroom facilitator and a student all at the same time, it is very easy to forget about all the surrounding politics that teachers themselves must navigate on a day-to-day basis. One of those is being pigeon-holed and, as a Black male educator, it is something that the PGCE experience really opened my eyes to because it gave me the chance to have a taste of the pressures of being an educator on a reduced timetable, whilst still having the opportunity for research and, most importantly, meaningful conversations with staff, students and parents.

Returning to how I first heard about the PGCE, it was through my headteacher at the secondary school where I served as a TA for roughly 4–6 months before I applied and enrolled on the course at the Institute of Education (IOE), part of the Education Faculty at University College London (UCL). My secondary school was extremely accommodating and all too keen for me to get 'stuck in' with supporting students in their reading, writing and exam technique. Well aware of what my ultimate ambition was, I asked which route into teaching meant I would be the least burdened with having to endlessly retrain before being able to 'country-hop' and, unanimously at the time, the answer was the PGCE route. This is what stoked my fire to excel as a TA in the beginning even more so because, coupled with my experience and a reference at the point of application, I was certain that if I proved I was capable of making a mark at this early stage, I would be able to truly make a difference anywhere I wished to go across the globe. But this was only my own perception of how my experience would 'serve' the school. As one of the largest secondary schools in East London, what they believed my brief tenure would bring was a 'reduction in apathy' amongst the 'most challenging' students who were susceptible to the allure of the 'fast life-style' advertised around them outside the confines of the school building. It did not take me long to register that this meant my time would largely be spent, in one instance, working almost exclusively with young Black boys who had been 'written off' as 'trouble-makers with no intent to learn', and it made me harken back to the portrayal of inner-city teachers in popular films who culled the class and built a protective bubble around the students they wanted to invest their time and energy in. The other students? They would be left to fend for themselves – unless someone who either resembled them, bore sympathy for the neglect they suffered within the classroom or, more powerfully, resonated with their experience because it was almost a 'shared trauma', made it their mission to intervene. Statistically, a young, Black English teacher of second-generation Nigerian descent is uncommon, borderline unlikely and yet here I was, unqualified at this point, facing a little apprehension from the group of students I was given to work with.

However, within a few weeks of consistently trying to establish a common ground with this group of students, they asked me a series of questions which I do not think they realised held a lot of weight at the time for me: 'Why would you want to teach this dead subject – you're Black, sir! Don't you think this subject is racist?' Another student joined in and shared his passion and asked me, 'So are you trying to be white? I thought you said you were Nigerian? Don't you think it's racist that they gave you us to teach?' Their questions were raw and honest, with a hint of disgust and disappointment coupled within the tone. Their main teacher, whose class I was supporting, taught me for A-Level so I was familiar with his lax approach to his students. At the time, the only immediate difference I could see between myself and those students was that I was determined not to be a statistic. Although they were preparing for their GCSEs at that time where they had allies as classmates, I stood alone many years before as the only Black boy in my class sitting that subject so I was resolved to outshine and outperform my peers. This was the ethos I wanted to instil within the students.

Now, I wanted to use this illustration to highlight how easy it is for trainee teachers and even more experienced teachers to become pigeon-holed into being 'transformational behavioural specialists' who 'rescue boisterous students and make them conform'. In any of the predominant routes into teaching but especially with the PGCE, what I believe is common-place is, if you are Black, the expectation is that you make the bad behaviour or non-compliance disappear because all too quickly you become relegated as ineligible for promotion later down the line. The assumption is, to continue my earlier war analogy, that if you are not equipped to survive in the 'trenches', then you will be unlikely to truly ever be able to do so when faced with even more adverse circumstances. Now, my PGCE year consisted of what I imagine for many is par for the course of any quintessential PGCE experience – the gruelling 3–4 month placements at two (usually) very different schools, the research assignments that are both similar and yet distinct from any experience at university and, of course, the snapshot the course provides into how the profession operates, inside and outside of your pedagogical practices.

The exact same unrelenting ethos of outworking your competition, regardless of how much sacrifice is required, is a dangerous trap to fall into as a PGCE student because of the array of hats you have to wear, as I have mentioned above. It is the exact one I fell into because I was so conscious of my surroundings: on my course, less than 5% of it was comprised of Black people, much less any Black men of which I was one of four. To make matters even more interesting, my first placement took place at a secondary school which boasted an intake of around 96% white teachers and students, located in a small town near Southend. For much of the PGCE journey, I felt either isolated, unknowingly measured by either prejudicial or down-right offensive assumptions or just simply observed through mystified lenses. But, one thing is for certain, after completing four assignments, planning and delivering my own lessons and actually creating schemes of work of my own and, most importantly, building relationships with individuals at the student, parent and personnel level within my two schools, I knew that the PGCE experience was the right choice for me because it allowed me to make mistakes without feeling completely burdened with the weight of thinking 'this is your class alone, you're failing them!' It allowed me to work collaboratively from day one, be creative, reflective, critical, and to balance proactiveness with assertiveness. But, most poignantly, the PGCE as a route into education made me consider:

1   Once I qualify as a teacher, should I fixate my gaze on just refining my planning and execution, suppressing that desire to retain the experimental side of 'learning to teach'?
2   Does being a student and a teacher for a short term and then being thrust with an enlarged teaching timetable weaken your ability to be a dynamic teacher?
3   Is the education system 'fixable' now with me in the mix or am I simply going to end up being made into 'another cog in the machine'? Now that is the question that I still wrestle with to this day, refusing to believe the former is impossible.

Shani Glover – Which route into teaching should I take?

Shani Glover is an assistant headteacher in a primary school. In five years, she has gone from being an unqualified teacher to a middle leader and now an assistant headteacher. Throughout her own journey as a pupil in school, so many teachers had a positive impact on her life; now she wants to be that person for future generations.

If I am honest, I didn't know what I wanted to do when I finished university. During my time at university, I worked as a Teach First Brand Ambassador, where my job was to encourage others to sign up to their postgraduate programme. I enjoyed working for Teach First and, ironically, I managed to convince myself to sign up to their Leadership Development Programme. Due to my role, I didn't have to fill out a long application; I was fast tracked to the interview stage – it just seemed to make sense. I'm sure we can all remember at least one teacher who made a real difference, who seemed to care that little bit more, who went that extra mile. As I went through the numerous stages, I knew I wanted to be that teacher; the one who went above and beyond for her students, an educator who made a real difference. I made it through the many rounds of the Teach First recruitment process and Summer Institute, and in August 2017 I set up my classroom and I knew I was ready! I like to think I walked into teaching with my eyes wide open – I knew it would be challenging, I knew my behaviour management needed to be robust and I knew that everything in a school was subject to change. However, training and being responsible for a whole class from day one is not an easy task. One thing I will say is that every school is different and some can be very supportive, whilst others buy into the notion that a Teach First teacher should be ready to teach from day one; in some cases, that expectation is too high for a young man or woman who just left university or a person who is career changing and has never worked in a school before. Teach First did prepare me to be a leader and the skills I learned on the Leadership Development Programme enabled me to have the confidence to move through leadership quickly. However, one issue with climbing the ladder so quickly and this fast-track approach to becoming a teacher is that you have to be willing to do your due diligence and consolidate your own understanding outside the classroom and in some cases even outside of your school. I am a strong advocate for Teach First. I believe in their social mission; their principles align with me as a person but to become a Teach First teacher you need to be very resilient – you need to walk into the process with your eyes wide open and under no illusion that your training years are going to be easy. I can promise that the impact you will have on the lives of young learners makes the process worth it!

I wish I had taken the time to research each pathway into teaching; on reflection, I wish I had done my due diligence and researched all aspects of education and the potential career opportunities. I can honestly say I fell into teaching; I don't regret it, as having the opportunity to help shape the lives of young people has changed me in so many ways. Nevertheless, had I known that my route was very independent and required me to reach out for support and seek additional CPD, I would have been better prepared. My hope is that through this chapter you will be better informed and it will help you decide which pathway best suits you.

Pathways into teaching: all of these routes require an undergraduate degree at 2:2 or above:

1   PGCE or PGDE at a University (student finance available)
2   School Direct (salaried and unsalaried positions, PGCE is funded)
3   Teach First (salaried and funded – entry requirement 2:1)
4   Postgraduate teaching apprenticeship

(Get Into Teaching, 2022)

PGCE or PGDE at a university

In most cases, you do not receive a salary on this route. You can apply for funding and for student loans to ease the burden; it costs around £9,250 for the year – in some cases, you can study part-time. Throughout the year, you are placed in at least two different schools, you are expected to complete assignments, collate evidence for each of the teaching standards and produce a professional portfolio – you will need to reflect on and journal your experience. Many find this route extremely supportive, and detailed; each step of the journey is explained, you have several peers to collaborate with, your university modules help to develop your pedagogy and your placements provide practical opportunities to implement what you have learned. Each university has its own course expectations and requirements, and it is paramount that you research the expectations of your desired university.

I felt supported from day one; I had the time, space and freedom to make mistakes and learn from them. (PGCE student, 2019)

School Direct

School Direct works with accredited teacher training institutions; you can undertake this route via university, London Diocesan Board for Schools (LDBS), or directly through partner schools.

While all three routes will provide you with a PGCE and QTS, whether you are salaried or not is school-dependent. If you undergo the route in conjunction with a university, in most cases you do not receive a salary – the LDBS offers both salaried and unsalaried, but their placements are for primary practitioners and are based in London. When applying directly to a school, make sure you read all the information; most schools will pay you, but it will be as an unqualified teacher (usually UQT1: £18,169–£23,099, depending on the location of the school). Via School Direct, you have a host school and your teaching commitment slowly builds from 10% to 80% across the course of the year. You are expected to complete assignments, collate a portfolio and complete a six-week placement. Practitioners often find this route gradually builds their confidence and subject knowledge, therefore they don't feel as overwhelmed by the process.

Teach First: Leadership and Development Programme (LDP)

This programme takes two years to complete and you are salaried from day one; upon the successful completion of the LDP, you will have obtained a Postgraduate Diploma in Education (PGDE) and Qualified Teacher Status (QTS). Whilst this route is salaried (UQT in the first year), the amount you are paid varies throughout the UK; it also varies in and around London. The LDP involves two placements, one in an alternate key stage and another in an alternate setting. The Teach First programme is designed for schools serving the needs of disadvantaged communities. Your placement school could be anywhere in the UK, though you can state a preference. Teach First begins with the Autumn Institute –

five weeks of training; this is designed to prepare you for the classroom, with the expectation being that you are ready to walk into your classroom at the end of October. Whilst some schools pair you with a partner teacher, the expectation is that this is your class – you are in charge of behaviour management, attainment, planning and delivering lessons, and it is your job to ensure your practice meets the needs of all children. When speaking to others who had chosen this route, the feedback was quite mixed, for instance:

> *In five years, I managed to climb from unqualified to an assistant headteacher. While I felt Teach First supported my development as a leader, I have found throughout my journey I needed to dig deeper and read more to develop my subject knowledge.* (Shani Glover, Teach First, 2017)

> *I found the programme challenging, I did not have the subject knowledge I needed; having the sole responsibility of the class from day one was too much. As a career changer, I was out of my depth; whilst Teach First supported my emotional wellbeing, there wasn't much they could do to support my day-to-day and I withdrew from the programme.* (Teach First participant, 2018)

Postgraduate teaching apprenticeship

This is a new route into teaching – not all routes allow you to obtain a PGCE, and many only offer QTS; if the PGCE is available, this often incurs additional costs. In some cases, the school will pay for it but make sure you have the conversation and everything is laid out from the beginning. This is a salaried route; you are employed directly by the school, however you split your time between the school and university. You are guided by an experienced teacher and expected to use at least 20% of your timetable to develop your pedagogy. The Department for Education has instructed schools to pay apprentices as an unqualified teacher; this is considerably higher than the apprentice minimum wage (£6.40 per hour).

Regardless of which pathway you choose, the culture of the school you are placed in is extremely important; if possible, try to visit the school beforehand. The benefit of the PGCE via university is that once the placement is over, you don't have to return. If you are in a school and you don't think it is the right fit for you, there are ways that you can request a transfer on the SCITT or Teach First programme, however this is not always guaranteed. Knowing how to collate evidence throughout your career is a great skill to have; if you request a transfer, you need a strong argument as to why. Keeping clear and concise records benefits your career too; you can use these to measure your impact and request a pay rise or put yourself forward for other progression opportunities. Each pathway is different and will bring about its own challenges; each career journey is unique and every one has its own story. Before you embark on this new chapter of your life, consider the following:

- What experiences do I already have in the classroom?
- How much support do I think I will need?
- Do I have a network of people to reach out to for support and CPD?
- Do I need to be on a salaried route?

Whichever path you choose, know that you are not alone and there is a network of educators rooting for you and here to support you if needed. Good luck, get ready and go for it!

Bibliography

Busby, E. (2016) Teach First easing workload to reduce drop-out rates. *Tes Magazine*, 9 September.

Get Into Teaching (2022) Train to be a teacher if you have or are studying for a degree. www.getintoteaching.education.gov.uk/train-to-be-a-teacher/if-you-have-a-degree (accessed 1 August 2022).

London Diocesan Board for Schools (2022) Train to teach. www.ldbs.co.uk/nqt-overseas-trained-teachers (accessed 10 August 2022).

NASUWT (The Teachers Union) (2022) Teachers' pay scales. Available at: www.nasuwt.org.uk/advice/pay-pensions/pay-scales/pay-scales-fringe-outer-london-and-inner-london.html#Unqualified%20Teachers (accessed 20 August 2022).

Teach First (2022a) Training programme. www.teachfirst.org.uk/training-programme (accessed 10 August 2022).

Teach First (2022b) What you could teach. www.teachfirst.org.uk/knowledge-base/training-programme/application/subject-availability (accessed 10 August 2022).

Teaching London (2022) School Direct Early Years Programme. www.teachinglondon.org/our-courses/school-direct-early-years (accessed 12 August 2022).

UCAS (2022a) Teach First Leadership and Development Programme. www.ucas.com/teaching-option/teach-first-leadership-development-programme (accessed 10 August 2022).

UCAS (2022b) Postgraduate Teaching Apprenticeship. Available at: www.ucas.com/teaching-option/postgraduate-teaching-apprenticeship (accessed 20 August 2022).

Big questions

- Are the current training programmes for potential teachers enough?
- Are there more ways we can consider to train teachers and to ensure they are equipped for the classroom in a way that will support them mentally, emotionally and financially?

4

Roles Outside of the Classroom

Caren

While the traditional classroom setting is where most teachers envision their careers, the skills and expertise we develop as educators translate incredibly well into numerous fields. This allows for teachers to cultivate their passion for learning and development in education-adjacent sectors. Sometimes these roles will be undertaken during your career as a teacher, and sometimes they will come during a career break, or if you choose to move on. There's no shame in choosing to do something else for a while and then coming back to teaching, or moving into a role where you utilise the skills you've worked so hard to achieve.

Education-focused career areas include:

- Curriculum and Assessment Development/Design: There's always the option of designing and assessing educational materials if you love planning and marking! Many teachers often work for educational publishers, e-learning platforms, the DfE, or directly upload their materials to platforms such as YouTube. Some become examiners or assessors for examination boards like AQA or Pearson, contributing to the development and marking of national assessments. During the recent Covid pandemic, many teachers worked on developing IT-based curriculum content, which could easily segue into roles in EdTech, product development and other IT-based arenas.
- Educational Consultancy: As an independent entity, a consultant can charge a daily/hourly fee for providing expertise to schools and other organisations. They may focus on specific areas such as teacher training or policy development.

- Museum/Arts Education: Teachers often move into roles in museums and other educational contexts when looking for a better work–life balance. You get the chance to create and develop educational programmes, lead tours and create workshops.
- Educational Policy and Advocacy: I toyed with the idea of going down this route, but felt I would miss the day-to-day interaction with students too much to move on. Teachers bring first-hand experience in the realities of classrooms, making their input vital for shaping policies that truly support students and educators. You can work with think tanks, advocacy groups or directly within government bodies as policy advisors for MPs, join education-focused think tanks, or become involved in local school governance as a school governor to influence educational legislation and decision-making. A good route into this is signing up for the policy roundtables often advertised through teacher training/development groups like Teach First.

Transferring your skills to a new environment:

- Corporate Training: The world of business offers opportunities for teachers to design and deliver training programmes for employees and management. Sometimes educational companies hire ex-teachers to design and deliver content that is tailor-made for their company.
- Human Resources: HR departments allow teachers to transition into roles that focus on employee development, onboarding, and training initiatives. Their background in assessment and facilitating growth for individuals is highly applicable.
- Nonprofit Organisations: Many nonprofits have educational components. Teachers can design and lead programmes, manage staff and create community outreach aligned with the organisation's mission. The charity I am currently a trustee for has employed countless people with previous experience in education.
- Project Management: Lots of my friends have left teaching to become project managers. I hear the pay is excellent! The organisational, time management and communication skills honed by teachers lend themselves to effective project management. This role spans industries, from tech to construction, where educators can guide projects to successful completion.

In conclusion, we need to acknowledge that the landscape of work is constantly evolving, and the core competencies of teachers – communication, collaboration, adaptability and a passion for lifelong learning – are in high demand across different sectors. Exiting the classroom doesn't equate to abandoning education.

It just broadens the reach of a teacher's impact and opens doors to new and fulfilling career paths. It also allows for the very important work–life balance we all seek. Teaching can be a job for life if you are still helping others learn and progress outside the classroom.

Kemi

I started off my career as a learning support assistant/teaching assistant and I made the assumption that the only other thing to do was become a teacher as I was very ignorant of other roles within education that were out there for pursuit if I wanted. I was under the impression that I would need a teaching qualification for any role in the world of education, which is not the case. Back in 2013 as a new graduate, I also did not think about roles in the education sector; I narrowly focused on classroom positions, but it is important for us to understand the many parts of the world of education that keep it moving. Over the course of my career, I've had the pleasure of meeting people who work in various roles that I didn't even know existed. These roles shape the world of education as we know it. These roles outside the classroom have an impact directly or indirectly on what goes on inside the classroom. Even as a SENCO, I never thought about working for a local authority or as a SEND advisor or as an education consultant. I did consider going down the pastoral route, but in the schools I worked in earlier on in my career, those roles were filled by teachers who had a reduced timetable and a Teaching & Learning Responsibility (TLR).

Some roles outside of the classroom that may be of interest are:

- Youth worker
- Project Manager
- Learning & Development
- Customer Success Manager
- School counsellor
- Pastoral manager
- Designated safeguarding lead
- Education consultant
- Education welfare officer
- Academic advisor
- Textbook writer
- School business manager
- Education manager
- Career counsellor/advisor
- Educational policy expert

I wished someone had sat me down and laid out all the different options that were out there for me to explore. I also should've done more research. Every role in education is important; it's like a jigsaw puzzle, with all the little pieces coming together to help us see the bigger picture and main focus, which are at the heart of what we do as teachers – the students.

Nana-Kofi Okyere – My journey into the wonderful and complex world of SEN

Nana-Kofi Okyere is a Senior Lead in a local authority, overseeing a SEN team, and a published author.

My journey into SEN started back in 2012 when I was at an interesting crossroads in my life. I had come out of the bubble of student life at university and was thrown into a world of bills, reality and more bills. At the time, I was convinced that I wanted to be a drama teacher full time. I had finished my undergrad degree in English literature with drama. Like most young adults, I was in a state of limbo after completing my degree. I worked in the drama department in my old school for a few months, supporting students that were doing their A-Levels. I really enjoyed it but it was voluntary, so I needed to find something that paid my phone bill and travel costs. The bank of Mum and Dad was now closed so I had to make my own money. I worked in different odd jobs from Poundland to Reiss to The Body Shop. After I quit my job at The Body Shop, I applied to work in an ASD school in East London. At the time, I didn't know it was an ASD school (a school supporting students with an autistic spectrum disorder diagnosis) and I didn't know what ASD was either. I just knew that my path was in education, so I applied to random schools until one of them got back to me. It just so happened that I got an interview at this school. I interviewed in the summer of 2012 and started working there in September of that year.

The first few days working there were a shock to me. I was a fish out of water. One of the young people I was supporting was having a meltdown and as I was trying to calm him down, I got slapped in the face followed by a gob of spit right after. At that point, with the phlegm dripping down the side of my face, I wanted to quit and go back to working at The Body Shop or go back to working voluntarily at my old school. But I had a chat with my team after that incident and, well, I just couldn't quit. Not just because I had to pay for my phone bills but also because I knew my path was to support these young people with significantly complex needs.

I was based in a class of eight children that were a mix of Years 10 and 11. Across the whole school, there were classes of no more than nine or ten young people.

Some classes had only six children, depending on how complex their needs were. The class I was in was labelled as a 'high-functioning' group in the school. They could communicate quite well verbally, and a couple of them could engage with the national curriculum and commute to school by themselves. However, each of them had difficulties with regulating their emotions, making friends and being able to communicate their needs. My role there as a TA was to help them in these specific areas. For example, encouraging them to work on tasks in small groups, looking at what friendship meant to them and what it looked like. I had to help them with their day-to-day education, whether it was maths, English, science or music. Their attainment levels were much lower than expected for their age, so the work was very different and tailored to meet their needs. I thoroughly enjoyed my two years there as a teaching assistant. I learned so much from working with these special children: learning communication systems such as Makaton, using Pecs and Symbols to communicate with non-verbal pupils or those with any other speech and language difficulties; learning how to deescalate situations with young people who are struggling to regulate their emotions; learning what different systems encourage them to improve in areas such as literacy and numeracy; and helping them build their self-esteem and learn independence skills. All of this was an important passion of mine, because I felt it was my duty to help them acquire skills to navigate the real world as they too will leave an educational system and have to face the realities of life whilst managing their autism or any other needs that they have.

After my brief stint as a teaching assistant, I was at another crossroads. One part of me wanted to go into teaching drama full time, but the other half of me wasn't done with SEN just yet. I still felt I had a purpose to serve in SEN, supporting young people. I applied to teach drama and I got onto the course but, at the last minute, I decided to apply to do a Master's in SEN. The beginning of my Master's course coincided with the introduction of the 2014 SEND code of practice set out by the Department for Education. The SEND code of practice details the legal and statutory obligations that organisations and professionals that work with children with SEN must uphold and follow without exception. It is the Bible of the SEN world, if you will. The system was transitioning from statements to EHCPs.

An EHCP is a document which outlines the educational, healthcare and social care needs of a child who requires additional support to help them access their education. The local authority has a statutory obligation to fund this additional support for every young person that has an EHCP, aged 0–25 years.

During the Masters, we covered a range of areas, specifically looking at the introduction of the SEND code of practice, the use of SENCOs, autism and behaviour. It was interesting coming from dealing with young people first hand, to looking at the theory behind the context of working with children with SEN – looking at the triggers that lead to challenging behaviours, how they process information and how they access their learning, amongst many other things. The course was fascinating and I picked up a lot of knowledge about SEN and the politics behind it. However, I am afraid to say that this could not prepare me for some shocking, harsh realities pertaining to the world of SEN in schools.

After my Master's was completed, I secured a job as a SEN case officer working for a local authority. My main role was to convert the statements on file to EHCPs. The DfE were moving from the old model of statements to EHCPs. The idea was that the EHCPs would have a more holistic view of the child and their needs, ensuring that the voice of the child was included and also the views of the parents, as well as identifying needs relating to social care, health and education. Part of my role was doing casework for schools, attending annual reviews and overseeing the 20-week assessment process.

One of the first things I discovered was that in order for things to run smoothly for young people, schools have to be inclusive and willing to make reasonable adjustments to meet the needs of individual children. Thankfully, some of the schools I worked with had this approach and they used the funding they got from the EHCP effectively to help the child meet the outcomes set out in their plans. However, I soon discovered that this was not consistent and some schools were using EHCPs as a ticket to get a child out of their school and into a special school, alternative provision and, in some cases, a pupil referral unit (PRU). Rather than using the EHCP and the money to support young people in these settings, it was turning into a conveyor belt for moving children with special needs out of mainstream settings. I attended countless annual review meetings where SENCOs and headteachers would state that they were unable to meet the child's needs. This put me in a compromising position because it meant that I then had to consult other settings for placement. The difficulty with this is that the recommendation of specialist settings should be coming from an educational psychologist and not the school; also, there is not an abundance of specialist settings and the ones that did tend to have spaces would be based far out of the borough. This puts an additional strain on the budget as the local authority has an obligation to pay for travel and, more often than not, the cost of an independent specialist placement is egregious, with some placements starting at £60k per year, not including transport.

One very sad issue that was all too common was the experience of Black families and their stance on the EHCP process:

- *Acceptance:* Always the first step, and understandably the hardest step for any family, no matter what colour they are, is accepting that your child has a specific diagnosis of SEN. The longer I have been in this arena, the more I have seen that young children are getting diagnosed a lot earlier. Early intervention can be seen as positive or negative. This is always up for debate. However, in my view, when it comes to Black families getting support, I feel that getting an early diagnosis and accepting the needs of the child early on is the best thing so that they can get the early help and intervention required.

One thing that isn't up for debate is that Black people generally start two steps back in the education system, so it is essential that any issues and concerns are addressed early on to give them a better chance to do well and progress. Many Black parents I have come across have had real difficulty accepting the reality of their situation where their child may have some additional needs. This could be due to pride, lack of knowledge, language barriers, or religious or societal ideals. Whatever the reason, refusing to accept that your child requires additional help will only set them back. Typically, speech and language input is more frequent and regular when a child is in Reception all the way up into Key Stage 3; after this, the support begins to reduce. Most speech and language therapists are of the view that their input is less effective as the child gets older and it is more important to get this support when they are in the early stages of development. So, if your child perhaps has a speech and language diagnosis and it is not addressed early on, it is likely that they will have a lifetime of these difficulties.

There are two particular issues here:

- *Lack of knowledge*: From my experience of working with Black families, there is a lack of knowledge of special educational needs, when it comes to what the needs of a child are. I have seen instances where parents have a child that has some sensory needs or some processing difficulties and they perceive them as being badly behaved or non-compliant, when this isn't the case. The child, more often than not, has difficulties navigating the environment they are in due to external factors. This could be related to touch, smell or sound. Anything in these areas can trigger a meltdown. Many parents don't do the detective work to get to the root cause of their child's behaviour. The solution to this simply is for parents to ask more questions of the SENCO, the educational psychologist, teachers and even teaching assistants, and to call for meetings to discuss the child's behaviour. The school has an obligation to put the needs of the child first, therefore this communication is essential. Unpack the issue and see if there are any patterns because after enough digging has been done, there will be some sort of pattern that has gone unnoticed. Parents need to do more reading and research on their child's needs. It doesn't hurt to explore this and even liaise with other parents that are in a similar situation. Too often, Black parents and families tend to isolate themselves out of shame or pride. The journey of having a child with additional needs isn't one that needs to be taken alone.

- *Discrimination*: This is a factor which sadly has an effect on Black people within the education system in this country. The statistics of young Black boys and girls being permanently excluded are at an all-time high. DfE data from February 2023 shows the highest permanent exclusion rates were for white Gypsy and Roma pupils (0.18%, or 18 exclusions per 10,000 pupils), and mixed white and Black Caribbean pupils (0.12%, or 12 per 10,000 pupils) (DfE, 2023). Black kids are always in the mix in regards to high exclusion numbers and, if nothing is done to target the practice of schools and the education system as a whole, they will always be in this mix.

I have sadly witnessed many instances where such children have been discriminated against. I saw a young boy, aged 8, who had a diagnosis of ASD and ADHD, arrested outside of the school. This young man was attending a PRU. He had a recent diagnosis and was in the process of getting an EHCP. He had had a meltdown in the school where he had lashed out at other pupils and staff so the school called the police. He was handcuffed and put in the back of a police car. This upset me greatly at the time and still saddens me to this day – that a young boy with such significant needs which he was born with, can be punished because of those needs, something which is out of his control. It amazes me and shocks me that with all of the training, experience and knowledge that the staff dealing with that situation had, they couldn't think of anything else to do but to call the police. Not to mention the thousands of pounds that the school had been receiving. Can you even begin to fathom the trauma and pain that this boy had to suffer? Being put into a police car as a child. It is heartbreaking to think of the amount of Black children with SEN that will face this level of discrimination on top of having very complex needs. They are not able to verbalise what and how they feel. This is something that needs to stop and I am afraid that the only way to stop it is if the system itself is destroyed and rebuilt. The fact that a young, vulnerable Black boy with ASD and ADHD can be put into the same box as a criminal is really concerning and even more disgusting.

This is just the tip of the iceberg. There are thousands of Black children in the UK with a range of additional needs that aren't receiving the sufficient assistance they require, whether it is due to resistance from Mum and Dad or the system being against them. All I can say is that the system needs to be reviewed from top to bottom, and we need more Black people in higher positions that can shake the table and make a difference, otherwise nothing will change.

Reference

Department for Education (DfE) (2023) *Permanent exclusions*. www.ethnicity-facts-figures.service.gov.uk/education-skills-and-training/absence-and-exclusions/permanent-exclusions/latest

Shamila Sulaiman – Sensational support staff: Realising a student's potential

Shamila Sulaiman is a UX consultant. She is also a playwright and director. Prior to entering the world of tech, Shamila worked as a probation officer and also in various support staff roles across four different schools. She is passionate about young people and paving the way for others to embark on careers in tech.

After studying psychology at university, I was convinced that I wanted to become a teacher. I will be completely honest with you; what attracted me most to the teaching profession were the holidays. I could not imagine what life would have been like without having a six-week break in the summer and having those Christmas and Easter breaks as well. Another thing that attracted me to the profession was my passion for young people. I attended an inner London school composed of people from different social strata. My experience in such an environment meant that I could identify with all kinds of students from all walks of life. Furthermore, when it comes to future aspirations, I am fully aware that there is sometimes a 'glass ceiling' limiting certain pupils, particularly Black people. So, as a teacher, I wanted to do something to negate this issue.

Unfortunately, when I went for my teacher training interview, I was told that I was 'too domineering' to be a teacher (whatever the heck that means!). Despite being disheartened at the time, I was determined to still work in the education sector. There are many ways in which you can have a positive impact on a student's life, particularly outside of the classroom, and I was determined to explore those options.

After being a teaching assistant for a year, I became a learning mentor. I was carrying out mentoring programmes and interventions for pupils who were working below their academic targets. I would do this through 1:1 mentoring and putting interventions in place throughout the academic year to make sure that targets were continuously met and fulfilled. Having attended several referral meetings and Pastoral Support Plan meetings, I understood the importance of referring students to the most appropriate form of support. Early intervention is key to ensure that a child succeeds, particularly for the Black students I worked with, as they were often seen as just 'troublesome'. I liaised with external agencies and organisations such as Targeted Youth, Functional Family Therapy, social services, youth offending teams and more.

As well as working with students who were referred to me for their learning needs, I also worked closely with students who had mild-to-severe behaviour issues. These issues often negatively affected their standard of work and behaviour for learning. At one of the schools I worked in, I was placed in the 'Fresh Start' department that worked with students who were unable to cope in mainstream lessons. Our aim was to minimise poor behaviour and exclusions and we did this by having a consistent, firm and fair behaviour approach. As you can imagine, there were many students who were faced with extremely difficult challenges, such as involvement in gangs, being neglected by parents/carers, and plenty of exclusions on their academic record. However, these students cannot be ignored; they were in dire need of support, and this was offered to them by our team.

In addition to this role, I became a careers coordinator and eventually a full-time careers advisor at another school. I remember when I was in school and having to see the careers advisor – it was the most pointless, most useless meeting I had ever attended. All I received was generic advice such as 'work hard'. I was adamant about creating an experience for young people that would not only be beneficial to them but could propel them in the direction that they wanted to take. As a careers advisor, I coordinated and managed the provision of Year 10 work experience, progression week and other career-related events. As horrendously tedious as it was, I worked tirelessly to place students in the most appropriate work placements. They weren't just placed anywhere, as I experienced when I was at school. I listened to their wants and desires, while also managing their expectations. I was able to grant them excellent placements, from GP surgeries to law firms to graphic design offices.

During 'progression week', I wanted to try something new and original. Thankfully, I have a great bunch of friends; all working in various industries. I brought them into my school for a career 'speed dating' activity where the students could meet professionals, ask them questions about their career path and gain insight into the world of work. I also created a Business Challenge. This one was my favourite! I grouped the Year 10 students into teams and they participated in an Apprentice-type business task. One year, students were required to create a new pizza from scratch, and design a new logo and pizza box for Pizza Express. The atrocities of pizza that I saw had me rolling on the floor, but it was the effort that meant so much to me. Some teams really put their foot in it (not literally, I hope) when creating their new pizzas but, of course, only one team could win. The winning team were given Pizza Express vouchers (courtesy of Pizza Express; thank you, guys!). Similarly, another cohort of Year 10 students was required to revamp the corporate identity of Nando's. They had to re-design and create a uniform, design a new logo and slogan, and produce a marketing campaign. We all took a trip to the haberdashery, and it was so heart-warming to see the dedication of all students, from the hand-drawn designs of the uniform to sewing it by hand. The winning team also won Nando's vouchers (thank you to the lovely manager at Nando's Canary Wharf for giving them to me). Overall, I was dedicated to facilitating career programmes for students that were both fulfilling and exciting. I saw a remarkable change in attitude displayed by some of the most challenging students. It was incredible to see the students flourish and become young adults through the challenges and tasks they had to undertake.

Whilst it sucked at the time that I couldn't become a psychology teacher, I was able to have a significant impact on the lives of hundreds of students. With a great team of teachers and other professionals, we raised the aspirations of pupils and encouraged them to consider the various choices that were available to them once they left secondary education. Not everyone is going to be a doctor or a lawyer. We need builders, we need software developers, we need beauticians, because we all know that when you look good, you feel good! Although I moved onto working in the criminal justice system and then into the world of tech, I am forever grateful for the students and professionals I worked with. Particularly the students; they inspired me so much! They exuded so much light and warmth. I still bump into many of my ex-students today and it is truly fulfilling to see them excelling academically and professionally. I pray that they have only continued success and happiness in their lives.

Big questions

- What else could be done to support students outside of the classroom?
- What else can be done to boost the profile of roles outside of the classroom and ensure those colleagues feel valued and empowered?
- Which roles am I missing in my school that could be of great benefit to the students we serve?

5
Black Men in Education

Kemi – Matter over mind?

Black male teachers make up less than 2.9% of the teacher workforce (DfE, 2023). Growing up, I didn't have as many male teachers as I did female ones and I definitely had no Black men who taught me until I got to Year 10. My business studies teacher was a Black man, a Nigerian who was also the Head of Business Studies. I also had a Black man who taught me chemistry for a short while, and there was a Black man who taught history, but he never taught me. So, in my seven years at secondary school/sixth form, I came across three Black men; that is a lot more than some have ever seen during their formal education and I was fortunate enough to at least be able to see them and be taught by two of them.

From talking to Black men and working with a few over the last 10 years, I have found that a majority of them were hired to fill pastoral roles and deal with or manage 'challenging behaviour'. I rarely heard of Black men who were hired for teaching and learning or any leadership roles that required strategic thinking and business ideas to support the running of the school. Their bodies and presence were used to deal with things other colleagues didn't want to deal with. We have read, heard and seen how Black men have been killed because people find them 'threatening' or 'intimidating', but I found it interesting that in the world of education and particularly in schools, the thing that 'scared' white people was the same thing some were using to their advantage in a school setting. That same 'intimidating' figure, stature or voice is what they wanted in place to keep students in line to reduce behaviour problems. It reminded me of one of my PE A-Level lessons where my teacher spoke about Black boys in America being used for their bodies rather than their intellect. This notion was also stated by Duffey, 2018: 'the social construct that depicts black athletes as physical specimens with natural ability and white athletes as witty and hardworking. The success of black athletes is often undermined by the notion that much of their ability comes naturally to them, and this ability allows them to overcome their lack of IQ within their given sport.' Yes, they are talented and gifted but the

Black body was reduced to its physical prowess on the basketball court and its brute force on the football field. As I did further research into this, it was also highlighted that intellectually successful Black individuals may be susceptible to being remembered as 'whiter' (SAGE Open, 2014). Those in higher places or positions of power that required strategic thinking, did not think that Black people had the mental ability or capacity for anything strategic or business related. I believe this is also reflected in the world of education, maybe not like it was 50 or 60 years ago, but it's still evident, not only in education, but in other sectors too.

References

Department for Education (DfE), (2023) School teacher workforce report [online], 6 July. https://www.ethnicity-facts-figures.service.gov.uk/workforce-and-business/workforce-diversity/school-teacher-workforce/latest/#by-ethnicity-and-gender (accessed 2 September 2024).

Duffey, Daniel E. (2018) 'It's No Secret, it's Racism', *Student Publications*. 689. https://cupola.gettysburg.edu/student_scholarship/689

SAGE Open (2014) 'Educated Black men remembered as 'Whiter' perpetuating stereotypes about race and intelligence', January 14, SAGE *Press Room*.

Caren – A rare breed: Black men in the British education system

Black male teachers in the British education system are a vital yet underrepresented group. The statistics paint a stark picture: only 3.5% of teachers in the UK are male from Black ethnic groups, compared to 85.8% who are white British (Black Men Teach, n.d.).

This underrepresentation has a significant impact on both educators and students, both in terms of role models and a support system. Adrian McLean (2021) aptly describes the situation in his online article for *Diverse Educators*, where he describes school days for Black boys as 'the worst time of their life. They didn't fit. Told they were trouble. Told they were stupid. Labelled. Written off.'

How then can we imagine this same young Black boy choosing – voluntarily – to walk and inhabit the same halls that traumatised him? The subconscious message that teaching and education aren't viable career paths for him has already been embedded. We are left with the chicken/egg paradox: what problem needs to be solved first – improving the educational experience of Black boys, so that they want to do the same for the next generation, or increasing the representation via superficial media campaigns, whilst doing nothing in reality to improve the experience of Black male teachers once they are through the door?

I am very lucky to work in a diverse school, where even amongst the senior leadership team we have lots of diverse representation. At the present moment, we have three Black male SLT members, two of whom have been in SLT for more than three years. This hasn't always been the case and it certainly isn't the norm in any school I've ever worked in across London.

Beyond visibility, Black male teachers often then have to navigate a landscape of microaggressions and stereotypes. Studies suggest Black teachers are more likely to be questioned about their qualifications or mistaken for non-teaching staff, as well as sidelined into roles within behaviour management and sports education (Hazlewood, 2021).

Despite the challenges, Black male teachers bring a unique perspective and valuable skills to the classroom. They can serve as positive role models for Black students, fostering a sense of belonging and academic confidence. Research suggests that Black students with Black teachers perform better and are less likely to be suspended (Black Men Teach, n.d.).

Organisations like Black Men Teach are working hard behind the scenes, alongside the Young Black Teachers Network (YBTN), to address the underrepresentation of Black male teachers. They provide support, mentoring, social connection, networking and leadership development programmes to equip Black men for a career in education.

The need for change is undeniable. A more diverse teaching force not only benefits Black students, but also creates a richer learning environment for all. By dismantling barriers, creating a welcoming environment and celebrating the contributions of Black male teachers, we can ensure that all students have the opportunity to learn from inspirational role models who look like and understand them.

References

Black Men Teach (n.d.) *Black Men Teach: The home for Black male educators* [online]. www.blackmenteach.co.uk (accessed 7 March 2024).

Duffey, Daniel E. (2018) 'It's No Secret, it's Racism', *Student Publications*. 689. https://cupola.gettysburg.edu/student_scholarship/689

Educated Black men remembered as 'Whiter' perpetuating stereotypes about race and intelligence, *January 14, 2014, SAGE Press Room*

Hazlewood, Y. (2021) I saw myself. *EqualiTeach* [online], 16 June. https://equaliteach.co.uk/i-saw-myself (accessed 7 March 2024).

McLean, A. (2021) A rare breed: The lesser-spotted Black male teacher. *Diverse Educators* [online], 21 January. www.diverseeducators. co.uk/a-rare-breed-the-lesser-spotted-black-male-teacher (accessed 7 March 2024).

Dami Iteye-Obi – I am more than just behaviour management

Damiebi Iteye-Obi is the lead advocate for Black Men in Education for Young Black Teachers Network (YBTN). His desire to break down the stereotype barriers that prevent Black men from progressing in the career of teaching has led him to deliver workshop events to aspiring Black male educators. Damiebi has 10 years' experience of teaching maths in inner London schools at middle leadership level. With this experience, he has helped mentor numerous trainees in achieving QTS.

My name is Dami and I am the Head of Maths at a secondary school in the UK. As a Black male in education, I have been exposed to the potential hurdles that sometimes prevent Black men from progressing to the top of the teaching profession. Having started my secondary school teaching career in September of 2014, I have experienced a steady but slow progression through the profession of teaching. This is of course due to many factors, however as a Black male teacher at times I have felt pigeonholed with the roles I aspire to attain. It is common in teaching practice that Black teachers are used as troubleshooters when dealing with badly behaved students. This is due to the stereotypes and perceptions regarding Black people being 'intimidating' or 'aggressive'. As a Black male teacher, I have been called upon to take on the more badly behaved because of these perceptions. While initially being willing to take on these more challenging classes, I have grown to learn that it is important to not let myself be seen as the teacher who is just good for managing behaviour. To do this, I started suggesting to the department that we all be behaviour management ambassadors. This meant that it was every teacher's responsibility to ensure they could manage any challenging behaviour in class. The suggestion ensured that all teachers, regardless of their experience, were accountable for the behaviour in their classes and along the department corridors.

The lack of Black male teachers is very well documented. There are a variety of reasons as to why Black men choose not to become teachers, one of which is the misinterpretation of how much teachers can earn. There is this notion that teachers do not earn a lot; now in comparison to high-end banking and accounting jobs, this is true but, in relative terms, teachers earn a good salary, especially those who work in inner-city schools. I believe that if the information regarding teachers' pay was made more accessible, then it would attract a lot more Black young men into teaching.

In my early years of teaching, I found myself trying to work almost three times as hard as my colleagues because I felt as though being a Black male teacher came with preconceptions that would cause others to not see the value in my practice. An example of this was when I had my first Year 11 top set exam group. The expectations and standards within my school are very high and having been given a top set exam group, I felt like there was a measure of pressure on me to ensure those top set students got amazing GCSE grades. Granted, I wanted to ensure my students got the best grades possible for my own personal accomplishment. I still couldn't help but feel as though I was put into a 'sink or swim' situation by the senior leadership team (SLT). As a result of this, I found myself staying back after school on multiple days to provide extra intervention lessons, in addition to doing drop-down days during the half-term breaks. This affected my work–life balance which at times caused me to question whether teaching was the profession for me. When the GCSE results arrived and my class got their outstanding results, it felt like a weight had been lifted from my chest. I finally felt like I had proven myself worthy, but was it worth the stress endured? Having had the time to reflect on this experience, I have concluded that as a Black teacher there will be times in your career where you feel like you must go above and beyond to get noticed; however, I am here to tell you that no matter what others may think, you are amazing. Always have confidence in yourself and know that, above all else, the students you teach will value your commitment and efforts, which is what counts the most.

Manny Awoyelu – The power of an educated Black man in school

Emmanuel Awoyelu is an educator, SENCO and former Assistant Head Teacher, currently working in the Middle East as an Inclusion Specialist Teacher and consultant. Emmanuel has spent the last decade working in both mainstream and special schools as a teacher and governor. He is also the director of the charity 'The reach out project'.

Growing up, I never associated Black people with teaching. This was particularly difficult to imagine in an area like Bermondsey, where the influence of the National Front was stronger than ever. I was 11 when I first saw a Black teacher. I had recently moved to East London and started secondary school in East Ham. Let's not be mistaken – there were far more white teachers than Black ones but it was still more than I had ever seen in one place. At least half of those teachers were men and the majority of them were of African heritage. The significance of these men being present in my school probably didn't hit me until I became a teacher in my early 20s. Each and every one of them had a part to play in my experience of school.

Mr B was a Black Briton like myself, of Nigerian heritage. I knew this because he had a Yoruba last name like mine and the head shape to go with it too. He walked with a swagger, had a gold tooth and was a real Cockney. He made it clear to us that he was 'one of the boys' in the way he spoke to us. However, even then, it was obvious it wasn't completely genuine. Eventually, it became clear he was trying to live up to something he thought we respected. He tried to be tough with us and remind us that he knew the roads and the ends just like us but this had the opposite effect. Very quickly, he struggled to command the respect he wanted from us, which eventually turned into a toxic relationship between many of my friends and Mr B. Even as 11-year-olds, we couldn't rate a teacher-wannabe-gangsta. We grew up around bad boys, so we didn't need a 30-something impersonating one of the mandem. 'Movee man' was the mindset we had for the remainder of our time at school when we saw him.

Mr C, on the other hand, was different. He was a gentleman. A Black male teacher who gained our respect without the bad boy vibe and without being a pushover. Unlike Mr B, he actually taught me, so my first interaction with him was as a student in one of his classes. I got to experience how much he loved teaching. He was smart, firm (but fair) and, more importantly, he was personable. He had the perfect balance. He quietly went about his business every day and, in the midst of teachers who struggled to gain our respect, we'd fix up in the corridors when we saw him. This is why it was difficult to stomach the news that he had passed away so quickly into our journey together. One sombre morning, we were all called to an assembly. It was unusual because assemblies were on a particular day, so we knew something was up but we never expected what we'd hear. A teacher stood up on the stage, took a deep breath and told us that Mr C had tragically passed away while on holiday during the holidays. He had suffered an asthma attack and left behind his newborn baby and wife. This may have been the first significant loss I had experienced. It was personal and it was the beginning of a collective type of trauma that would follow me for years to come.

As I muddled through secondary school, there was one teacher in particular who left an imprint on my life. It was Mr O. I'll never forget Mr O because we gave him hell on his first day as a supply teacher in our science lesson. I think I respect him more because he kept coming back. I remember our first interaction like it was yesterday. I sat in the science lab, waiting for a teacher to arrive. It had been at least five minutes and no one showed up. People were throwing paper planes, a mini fight had broken out in the corner of the classroom, children were jeering; it was anarchy. I decided to get up and stand in the middle of the class and... well... I'll save the rest for another day. It's just important to know that Mr O walked into the classroom at that very moment. My back was facing the entrance so I didn't see him enter the room. It went deadly quiet, followed by sniggering. I made eye contact with my friend who raised his brow and I knew a teacher was standing behind me. I didn't even waste his time. I picked up my bag and quietly walked out of the class. That was the beginning of a topsy-turvy relationship with Mr O.

I couldn't stand him in the beginning. I thought he was strict and obnoxious. Just like me, Mr O was Nigerian, but not a Black Briton. He was a tall, serious man with an air of mystery about him. He was trained in some form of martial arts and even showed us some moves when we teased him. Most of our time with Mr O led to him giving us lectures. He'd remind us that the system wasn't designed for us to flourish and that we needed to work smarter and harder than our white counterparts. You could tell he really cared about us and he didn't want us to waste our lives. On one particular occasion, he was so angry with me and my best friend that he completely ripped into us. For once, we had nothing to say. We knew we had let him down. I knew Mr O meant business when he threatened to call our dads and that was exactly what he did. One time he did it in a lesson. Hearing him speak Yoruba to my dad made my head hot because I knew and everyone else knew what was coming when I got home. He single-handedly gave my dad insight into my school life as well as trust in one of his son's teachers. It reminded me of the kind of relationship I had with the grandparent of a former student. A year after leaving school, my best friend and two other school friends tragically passed away in a car accident. When we held a memorial for them in a church close by, Mr O surprisingly showed up. He stood at the back of the church and when I saw him, the words he spoke to me and my best friend just two years prior rang loud in my head. I went to say hi and he embraced me like a father would his son. In that moment, I could feel his pain.

Unfortunately, it was maybe a little too late to change the path I was on when Mr O joined my school but I was recently reminded that it was never his sole responsibility to safeguard me and ensure I left school with the right tools to succeed in life. This needed to be a shared effort and, in my case, I was failed by the wider school system. Nonetheless, the impact of these men should not be understated. In their own way, they all individually gave me an experience that I would want to share with my pupils. I want my students to see me and see someone from their community, I want them to feel valued and I want them to feel like they have an advocate. In a sector that is heavily dominated by women, it's important we are visible so that the narrative of the educated Black man can be normalised. We belong in these spaces just as much as anyone else. This is why I'm encouraged by the work of the Young Black Teachers Network and Black Men Teach. By amplifying the voices of Black male educators, we can change the narrative and the outcomes for young Black boys in Britain.

Massimo Ampofo – A Black male's journey into teaching

Massimo Ampofo is a secondary English teacher currently working in a British international school in Dubai. As a pastoral leader, his principal aim is to help all his students become open-minded, global citizens. By extension, he is particularly passionate about reframing dated and toxic ideas on masculinity.

I never wanted to be a teacher. In fact, once upon a time I could think of nothing worse. My secondary education was earned in a comprehensive Catholic boys' school in East London. While it was known primarily for academic and sporting excellence, it was also known for having a 'unique' pupil base. My classmates tended to be ethnic minorities that hailed from socially deprived areas. Their challenging circumstances meant that many of them displayed challenging behaviour at school. Teenage insecurity and peer pressure being what they are, I also, at times, engaged in misbehaviour myself. Boisterousness and altogether toxic masculinity were a way of life.

For us, it was all fun and games when somebody got hurt – especially teachers. We had plenty of excellent teachers that we knew not to cross. But if ever there were one incapable of inciting fear, we would run them ragged. They would be objects for our amusement; the centre of laugh-filled conversations for years to come. I remember one teacher in particular that me and my peers, essentially, bullied for a term. Knowing that there was only so much he could mete out as consequence, we set out to provoke him. It eventually got to the point where one day he lost all composure and shouted until he turned completely red. The worst thing was that he did not even shout at me, even though I had been the main culprit. Instead, he picked on an innocent in what was a clear attempt to rescue face. For me, it was an egotistical victory. I laughed as I left the class that day, proclaiming loudly 'that could never be me!' Funny how life has a way of making you reap what you sow...

Aside from being at the mercy of cocky pubescents, I also did not fancy teaching because of the lack of prestige I associated with the role. As an academically capable student, I was told by many of my teachers that I would go on to do 'big things'. I always assumed these 'things' would be of national consequence, or, at the very least, beyond the scope of the classroom. I have often reflected on why I used to minimise the role of the teacher in this way and tended to arrive at the same conclusions. Firstly, I feel my teachers are partly culpable; in making such comments about my future, they essentially portrayed themselves as nothing more than humble stewards of my potential. The truth is, they were much more. However, perhaps more significant is the attitude of my parents. Now, for the avoidance of doubt, my parents were always supportive of my professional aspirations. But, having come to the UK from Ghana, they had a very narrow view of what 'aspiration' looked like. To them it looked like one of three things: doctor, lawyer or engineer.

For my parents, these three careers represented the apex of social and financial status. They were bragging tools and even bargaining chips amongst friends and family (Nigerian traditional wedding, anyone?). My parents themselves had only ever worked in blue-collar jobs throughout my childhood. They came from humble beginnings and lived through periods of economic and political unrest between the 1970s and 1980s. Their life experience meant that they valued job security above all else. These industries, which represented a far removal from my parents' own careers, guaranteed security throughout one's working years – and a nice retirement scheme to boot. As far as they were concerned, being a teacher held no such promise.

I cannot blame them. Self-indulgent phone calls back home aside (normally to Sister Aggy), my parents just wanted what was best for me. It was the same for most of my friends as well. Unfortunately, everybody thinking this way also created another barrier of entry into teaching: nobody in the game really looked like us.

I was fortunate to have personally been taught by three Black teachers whilst at school. But, if anything, that only further highlighted our lack of representation in the industry. Because every other teacher was white (and predominantly male), my friends and I found ourselves clambering desperately for that bit of Blackness. The main reason I chose graphic design for my GCSEs was not because I was particularly good at it; it was because the course teacher was a Black man. He was also a phenomenal teacher, too, but that was a bonus! I just intrinsically knew that I needed the guidance of a Black male in school.

One of the things that made my graphic design teacher so endearing was the sense that he was 'repping' for us on his own. He made us feel seen and in so doing filled us with immeasurable pride. But I think this may have inadvertently played a part in me and my peers feeling even more like teaching was not for us. I believe it was the perceived loneliness of it all. Teenagers are uncomfortable having their differences highlighted at the best of times. To wilfully make the choice to be the 'token' seemed to us to take real strength of character.

I am glad to know that, ultimately, I possess such strength. Having been in the profession for almost 10 years now, I know that increased representation in this field is paramount. To advocate for the needs of our children, we need to be in the spaces they spend the majority of their time. It is how we normalise diversity. It is how we enable fairer and more representative education. It is how we prevent (or at least bring about justice for) 'Child Q'. This need remains even in international environments. I have been teaching in international schools since 2016 and Black people still tend to be the overwhelming minority in these spaces. Whether fortunately or unfortunately, there is no shortage of need.

Big questions

- How comfortable are you with the idea of being Black in a predominantly white space?
- How might you use your own Black experience to help a young Black person understand their own?

6

Black Women in Education

Caren – Misogynoir: Where racism and sexism meet

Misogynoir, a term coined by Moya Bailey, describes the unique intersection of anti-Black racism and misogyny that Black women experience. In her book *Women, Race and Class* (1981), Angela Davis examines how interlocking oppressions create a distinctive set of challenges for Black women in all fields, including education. Mainstream feminism has often ignored this intersection of race and gender for Black women (Anyangwe, 2015), thereby leaving it to the women who are themselves marginalised to explore the field.

Whilst completing my MA in Contemporary Literature in 2015/16, I was struck by the lack of broad representation of Black female role models in educational literature. If what we are feeding into our collective minds through various media (think *The Real Housewives of Atlanta*, adverts, social media and the aforementioned school texts) reinforces negative stereotypes, how can we expect the resulting perceptions of Black women to be positive? If the stories always end in tragedy, or triumph against extreme adversity, how can we raise Black women to expect, receive and enjoy soft lives? Do we even believe we/they deserve it?

As I wrote my final thesis on this exact topic, I mused on the limited tropes and roles we are given:

- Sapphire: hard, rude and sassy. Archetypal bad gal/angry Black woman.
- Mammy: podgy and sacrificial. Always feeding and caring for others.
- Jezebel: sexy, promiscuous and immoral. Characterised by the '90s video vixen.

Are these characteristics unique to the Black race? No. Are Black representations of these caricatures perpetuated across mainstream media? Yes (West, 2008).

If young people from a range of backgrounds are fed these stories and roles, is it any wonder they quickly fall into line when in large groups? Is it any wonder that young people of all races rush to these stereotypes when describing Black women? Despite each girl's individual lived experience, these tropes follow us throughout our lives and can lead to extreme confusion in our colleagues if we don't fit the brief. Having spent the majority of my life in white communities, I had grown accustomed to expressing the whole gamut of emotions. There was one occasion when I cried when I was upset and a colleague of mine almost chastised me for expressing emotions. I had to politely remind her that I was human and that when humans are upset, they often cry. This wasn't a high stakes situation in front of high-powered stakeholders; this was me expressing sadness that a boy in my year group had just been permanently removed from the school due to his underworld connections.

It's important we encourage young Black girls to be fully expressive (in and out of school) and encourage this translation into self-expression through whichever field or medium they feel most comfortable in. We need to normalise Black women as being women first, Black second. This will hopefully contribute to the shifts in society we need to see and increase positive representation both within and outside education.

Despite their limited numbers, Black women have played an essential role in shaping education in the UK. Their contributions extend from breaking barriers and championing inclusion, to enriching the educational environment for students across backgrounds. This journey, however, is deeply intertwined with the ongoing struggle against misogynoir, underscoring an added layer of complexity to the fight for equity and representation.

Pioneering figures like Yvonne Conolly, the UK's first Black headteacher in 1969, made history despite the challenges she faced. The Windrush generation, which included Williams and many other educators, established organisations like the Caribbean Teachers Association (CTA) to advocate for Black educators and celebrate heritage within the educational sphere. Yet, the underrepresentation of Black women in leadership positions remains evident: according to the National Association of Head Teachers (NAHT), the statistics suggest a mere 1.2% of headteachers identify as both Black and female (DfE, 2023). In real terms, that's fewer than 200 Black female headteachers, from a pool of over 14,000 female headteachers and over 20,000 headteachers overall in England. A drop in the ocean.

So, what's the solution?

The work of educational researchers such as Cui and Ankrah (see, for example, Cui, 2016) calls for anti-racist and inclusive educational practices. Increasing the representation of diverse voices across disciplines, including education, remains crucial. Celebration of the successes of Black women in UK education is also essential, so that we can encourage the next generation(s) of empowered leaders and their allies.

References

Anyangwe, E. (2015) Misogynoir: Where racism and sexism meet. *The Guardian*, 5 October. www.theguardian.com/lifeandstyle/2015/oct/05/what-is-misogynoir (accessed 7 March 2024).

Cui, D. (2016) Teachers' racialised habitus in school knowledge construction: A Bourdieusian analysis of social inequality beyond class. *British Journal of Sociology of Education*, 38(8): 1152–1164.

Davis, A.Y. (1981) *Women, Race and Class*. New York, NY: Random House.

Deparment for Education (DfE) (2023) *School teacher workforce*. www.ethnicity-facts-figures.service.gov.uk/workforce-and-business/workforce-diversity/school-teacher-workforce/latest.

West, C.M. (2008) Mammy, Jezebel, Sapphire, and their homegirls: Developing an 'oppositional' gaze toward the images of Black women. In J.C. Chrisler, C. Golden and P.D. Rozee (eds), *Lectures on the Psychology of Women*, 4th edn (pp. 287–299). New York, NY: McGraw-Hill.

Kemi – Always on edge

As a Black woman, I'm hyper aware of the tone and pitch of my voice, facial expressions and body language as I don't want to be labelled as the 'angry Black woman'. I'm aware that what a member of staff of a different race can get away with saying or doing, I don't have the same luxury, so I have to be careful. If I was direct, I was rude. If I was passionate about a topic, I was aggressive. If I was upset about something someone did or said to me, I was being oversensitive and needed to calm down.

I had a colleague who was not happy that as her manager I needed her to complete a task that would take a few minutes, but told me it would take four working days. When I offered to do the task myself as it was a very quick and straightforward thing to do and I couldn't wait four days, it had to be escalated and the same colleague had every excuse under the sun as to why she couldn't do what I had asked her to do. This same colleague spoke to me in a very rude manner on more than one occasion and in front of students, and I had to bite my tongue more than once to avoid the stereotype. But how much can one person take? In the end, I made it clear that she should never speak to me like that again.

I walked away and went about my day, only to be told 20 minutes later that the colleague was in tears and felt attacked. The word 'attacked' was the icing on the cake for me. If only I had weaponised my tears earlier when I had been disrespected, maybe people would've felt sorry for me as well and the task that needed to be done, would've been done sooner.

I've always felt that what I do or didn't do will be scrutinised to a different level compared to colleagues who were not Black. I learnt from a young age that my skin colour, my Nigerian name and being a woman could be a hindrance in the working world. What the world was telling me was that I wasn't enough and the people who looked like me weren't good enough. I have witnessed amazing Black women work hard to be promoted or go for a role that they were more than qualified for, but those same women were overlooked and the role was given to someone who wasn't Black and wasn't as qualified or experienced. I've spoken to other Black women who also experienced being ridiculed for not speaking a certain way and received various comments on how they chose to wear their hair.

I'm proud of my culture, my Nigerian heritage, skin colour and name (I will correct people every single time they pronounce my name wrong). I'm happy with the way God made me. Even when things have been difficult, it's moments like when I had some Year 11 students tell me how happy they were to see someone who looked like them represented in the senior leadership team, that made me feel like I was doing the right thing. It warmed my heart because although I had a couple of Black women who taught me when I was in school, I wished it was the norm. I was glad that as a Black woman in education, I could be the visible difference and make a difference in the hope that my children won't have the same conversations or feel the same way in the next 10, 20 or 30 years.

Alison Kriel told me to work in a school where I can be my authentic self and reminded me not to compromise on who I am, especially as a Black woman. The 'strong Black woman' stereotype can often follow us as well and it's perfectly OK to be strong, but it gets tiring. I'm human and I'm fragile too. I've had to learn to ask for help when I need it and not feel like I have to carry everything and be everything. I'm still learning this and part of that learning is trusting others to do their job, but sometimes I feel it's just easier to get things done on my own rather than waiting on people. As stated in Ramdeo's 2023 paper on the experiences of Black women educators, 'Black women tend to be seen through harmful stereotyping and controlling images such as "Mule" (bearing the burden of additional workloads) "Mammy" (motherly, nurturing, yet strong disciplinarians), "Sapphire" (loud, dramatic), "Crazy Black Bitch" (angry, aggressive, unstable) and "Superwoman" (over-achiever, can handle large workloads without complaint) which continue to be pervasive in the workplace As such, Black women's non-prototypicality creates invisibility that impacts on their career trajectories and wellbeing.' (Ramdeo, 2023: 5)

I haven't always felt that I could be my authentic self in a room where I was the only Black person. Of course, even if I am, I will still hold my head high and do what I need to, but there's something about having other Black women around and genuinely supporting one another that makes carrying the load lighter. Maybe it's a cultural thing; being able to connect with someone that you see as a friend, sister, aunt or work-mother type figure. All I know is, it has made a difference for me and I haven't always felt alone.

I'm grateful for the Black women I've had the pleasure of working with and learning from. I'm grateful for the lessons I've learned in order to protect myself, do my best, get support when I need it and also show up as my authentic self, whether I'm teaching, meeting with parents, external agencies, the senior leadership team or the board of governors. I will always stay true to who I am and do my role to the best of my ability.

Reference

Ramdeo, J. (2023). 'Black women educators' stories of intersectional invisibility: experiences of hindered careers and workplace psychological harm in school environments'. *Educational Review*, 1–20. https://doi.org/10.1080/0013 1911.2023.2217358

Alison Kriel – Holding on to self

Alison Kriel was an inner-city executive headteacher for nearly 20 years and a CEO for 5 years, leading her schools to be in the national top 100 and highest performing in London. She now works nationally and internationally, supporting leaders. She is a regular keynote speaker, speaking on a wide variety of subjects including conscious leadership, Turnaround schools, the unmeasured curriculum, the global curriculum, appreciative inquiry, wellbeing, staff retention, intersectionality, breaking through the concrete ceiling, equity, diversity and inclusion, Ubuntu and anti-racism.

Alison is the founder of the newly launched Above & Beyond Education – a social media platform for all educators and schools to celebrate, connect, support, grow and collaborate to make every school into a great school.

In the early days of being a CEO, I recall being invited to a Department for Education event bringing female CEOs together to discuss encouraging more women into a role within education, as there were only 0.05% female CEOs in a workforce that was 80% women.

Guests spoke powerfully about their leadership journey and the barriers they overcame, the Equalities Team presented data confirming the lack of representation, and there was plenty of discussion about narrowing the gap. It was an important day of unity, and at the end I went to thank the Equalities Team and Regional Schools Commissioners for the day. I pointed out that I was the only Black person in attendance and that I was surprised intersectionality was missing on the agenda. The response took me by surprise: 'We didn't know we had a Black CEO until you pitched up today.'

The truth is that statistical data about gender and race is not collated beyond headship level and there is no desire to do that. This may well be because the statistics don't look good.

DfE data shows that in 2019:

- there were around 22,400 headteachers in 2019, and over two-thirds of those (around 15,100) were women
- 96.1% of female headteachers were white (92.6% White British, 1.7% White Irish, and 1.8% White Other)
- 97.0% of male headteachers were white (92.9% White British, 2.1% White Irish, and 2.0% White Other)
- 89.7% of our Deputies and Assistant Heads are white. There is an overrepresentation of Black women who are Heads of School, which effectively means that there is an acknowledgement that these women can lead and can do the job, but they are not allowed to be paid for the work that they do and have no authority to make strategic decisions.

Our challenge is that we don't fit stereotypes around how leaders look and act. Gender and leadership is widely researched, but the complex intersectionality of the Black woman leader is less so. When we think leader, we think male. When we think of a female leader, we think white woman. When we think Black women as leaders, then colourism, hair type, size, shape and age become a critical part of why we are not appointed. Once appointed, our Blackness is always on display – our hypervisibility means we try to adapt our look, our tone, our success, to ensure we don't contribute to the discomfort of others.

I recall going for my first headship interview, and being told that if I really wanted the job I needed to look the part by blow drying or relaxing my curls so that my hair was straight and more European, and I had to wear a suit. I needed to take on the attributes of a man in a suit and change my appearance to look as white as possible. It was deeply uncomfortable. I played the game on the first day, but on the second I wore a smart dress and allowed my hair to be natural. I had a clear vision on the school I wanted to run, clarity on the journey I would take the school through (I was the founder headteacher of a new school) and I was determined to uphold my integrity by being true to myself. I decided to be an expert in my own cultural capital rather than take on the cultural capital of a group that I knew I could never be a part of. If the governors were not willing to accept me as I was, then I did not want to work with them. I knew I was an unconventional leader who would be placed under close scrutiny and I could not afford to make mistakes. I believe that one of the reasons I was successful in getting the job was because despite the challenges, I faced the fear and did it anyway, refusing to compromise who I was. I then ensured every promise I made regarding the development of the school was kept. My mantra: failure was not an option.

A big challenge for Black women leaders is to be a strong, assertive and intentional leader without being perceived as a threat to the white majority. As a community, we have much to celebrate but, as in all leadership, we have our share of lows too. I had to find a way to navigate challenging times without expressing disappointment, anger or hurt. I could not afford to be labelled as 'the angry Black woman'. A male leader dealing with challenges is seen as assertive. A white woman, passionate. A Black woman becomes the angry Black woman. In the best of times and the worst of times, I smiled, remained calm, buried my feelings and became increasingly hyper-independent. My external calm suggested everything was under control, despite everyone knowing that school leadership is fraught with challenges. It was an extremely lonely and unhealthy way to survive.

As a Black person, these are prerequisites to success. When you are a leader, you go through the same range of emotions as everyone: joy, pride, hurt, anger, irritation, fear. It is emotionally exhausting, yet the Black female leader has to find ways to navigate their way through expressing calm, quiet, unassuming assertiveness because we don't fit in with everybody's model of leadership and it's easy for observations of our emotions to be used as ammunition against our inability to cope.

Governors in my first headship worked hard to micro-manage my every move. It was a middle-class, white community and from conversations with other headteachers, I could not help but notice parents over-scrutinising everything I did and signalling their power by taking everything to the governors rather than talking directly to me, and the governors indulged them. I had to be over-accountable for everything. The headteachers in my nearest schools, serving the same demographic, were white men and were never questioned or held accountable in the same way. Adding to insult was knowing that I was the lowest paid headteacher in my local authority, despite exceeding every performance target, having high pupil attainment and excellent Ofsted ratings, and being the most popular school in the local authority, as reflected in having the longest pupil waiting list. When questioned, I was told it was because I was young. Every other headteacher was paid based on the performance management cycle.

By the time I started my second headship and the role of executive headteacher, I had learned the importance of finding my voice and speaking out, even when my knees are shaking. I continued my commitment to always doing an excellent job and delivering on promises.

My second headship was in a school which had been badly neglected by the local authority. It was the Black, working-class school, the lowest performing in the borough, and nationally too. There was a failure in duty of care of the community by the local authority and a lack of investment. Now, hindsight is a beautiful thing. When I was asked to take on the second role, I was seen as a highly successful leader running a successful school. I had started to find my voice and spoke out about the 12 out of 17 Black headteachers who had either been dismissed or 'disappeared'. I thought I was asked to support it because the work in my first school was valued and I felt flattered by the invite. I now know that it was because it was an opportunity for me to be pushed out. My success was seen as a threat and speaking out about injustice made me a greater threat to those in authority. The local authority was in crisis as the lowest performing in the country with a high number of failing schools. Black leaders, who often had to apply for 10 or more headships prior to being appointed, were recruited in their failing schools. By the time they applied, they were worn down by rejection and driven by getting the role rather than being selective on settings which would invest in their success. They were new headteachers and there was no mentoring programme in place, no scaffolding for the community, and unrealistic turnaround targets. When I was asked to take on the failing school, it was an interim four-month arrangement and I kept my promise by getting the school through a challenging Ofsted inspection. I was then invited to stay for longer. Other heads in the local authority when overseeing two schools, were called Executive Heads; I was asked to be an Associate Head. I rejected the title. I was asked to turn the school around in one year; I committed to three. I became the classic Black woman who was about to be penalised for my excellence which was always a threat to the status hierarchy. Black women leaders are not permitted to be self-promoting in their ambition. I heard time and again that the directorate thought I was after the Director of Education role, even though I made it clear that my passion would always be for working directly in schools.

We were over-scrutinised! Other schools were audited every three to five years; ours every one to three. We had a red flag on one occasion as I bought a bunch of flowers for a member of staff, who had spent her weekends and evenings making costumes for a nativity play. I used the school credit card to buy her a bunch of discounted flowers in Morrison's. It was less than £10.00 and a pupil was asked to give them to her on the last night of the show. Meanwhile, I heard stories of a white headteacher in a nearby school using a large amount of school funds for something only very loosely school related – by most accounts far more personal – yet only marked as an orange in the audit report. We had termly 'mocksteds' and all our SATs were moderated, whilst other schools were moderated every three to five years. I got to the point of calling the local authority to enquire who would be coming so that we could get their favourite biscuit in. We treated it with humour to mask our anger at the bias which was clear for all to see. But the benefit of hindsight is valuable and I can now see that all that over-scrutiny of our data, finances and procedures ratified our excellence.

I stuck to the rules solidly to keep myself safe. I couldn't just prove my competence, I had to excel. And all the while, I remained very calm and very quiet, even when people were at their very worst, to avoid the angry Black woman label. I was conscious of research which showed that female employees who expressed anger were conferred lower status and salary compared with 'authoritative' male employees. In short, Black women's power to control their own actions is restricted, whilst white men who take up their power are rewarded through pay and promotion.

Self-belonging is integral to self-esteem, life satisfaction, mental wellness and an increased likelihood of reaching our full potential. If you can't be your own authentic self, it's only a question of time before the preoccupying fear of failure sets in. Learning to be unapologetically me was probably part of my empowerment. I recognised that no matter what I did, I was never going to be at my best if I took on the cultural capital of a white person.

Black women often find themselves embraced by the organisation when they first take up post. However, there is a recurrent pattern that many find themselves in as soon as the honeymoon period is over.

In 'The Time For Talking Is Over, Now Is The Time To Act', the McGregor-Smith review into Race in the Workplace, it was found: 'There is discrimination and bias at every stage of an individual's career, and even before it begins. From networks to recruitment and then in the workforce, it is there. BME people are faced with a distinct lack of role models, they are more likely to perceive the workplace as hostile, they are less likely to apply for and be given promotions and they are more likely to be disciplined or judged harshly' (DBIS, 2017). I am frequently asked what actions Black women can take to overcome these barriers.

Based on my own personal experience, I believe:

- that rather than negotiate imposed identities, we take up our authority to have our own cultural capital accepted, respected and valued
- we should appreciate the value of mentorship and take up responsibility for finding a mentor who will champion us, hold us to account and provide a safe space for decompression
- we can prioritise working in places where we are accepted for who we are, rather than getting the right job title in a place where we will have to diminish ourselves to fit in
- change from the middle only leads to tensions, so seek out leaders who take responsibility for developing their racial literacy and make it transparent through their organisational practice. It is not our responsibility to rescue the institution nor to lay our own personal experiences bare for others to feast on at our expense.

Bibliography

Coco-net (n.d.) *The 'Problem' Woman of Colour in the Workplace.* https://coco-net. org/wp-content/uploads/2018/03/WoC-in-Organizations-Tool-FINAL-EN.pdf.

Department for Business, Energy & Industrial Strategy (DBIS) (2017) *Race in the Workplace: The McGregor-Smith Review.* www.gov.uk/government/publications/ race-in-the-workplace-the-mcgregor-smith-review.

Worth, J., McLean, D. and Sharp, C. (2022) *Racial Equality in the Teacher Workforce: An Analysis of Representation and Progression Opportunities from Initial Teacher Training to Headship.* Research Report. National Foundation for Educational Research (NFER).

Sarah Adenuga – The loneliness of leadership in outer London schools

Sarah Adenuga is an English teacher and experienced senior leader with success in teaching and learning roles, as well as pastoral. Having worked in schools of varying demographics, from London to Essex, she is passionate about inclusive practice and social justice.

Having started my teaching career in an inner-city, London secondary school, the concept of being a Black woman never occurred to me. For instance, we had a Black headteacher and the staff were extremely diverse. This consciousness of being a Black woman finally occurred when I was offered a role in extended leadership in a school in Essex.

My first day at the school is a vivid recollection. I started with another young lady in the English department, who was white. The reception she received was in stark contrast to mine. She was welcomed with a smile, whereas I was completely ignored. The ethnic make-up of the school and local area was white British. Being a minority felt like an isolating experience and it didn't help that my classroom was situated on the opposite side of the building, far away from the English department. I was the only English teacher that was put there. My first year at the school continued to be a lonely experience. Every Friday evening was a pub night. The invitation never extended to me. I learnt about Friday pub night when they would converse about it in the English office.

This was the first of a few interesting experiences. The first school Christmas party I attended was held in a local pub. Many had consumed enough alcohol to make them merry and sociable. A few of us were on the dance floor, when Kanye West's *Gold Digger* song started playing. Based on my experience already with the staff in the school, an unsettling feeling trickled through me. My instincts did not fail me. Kanye's voice rings out of the speakers, singing the chorus with 'the n-word'.

At this point, one of the English teachers began pointing directly at me whilst singing along to that word. This was the first of a few overt and covert racist interactions. These included comments such as: 'I can't keep up with your hairstyles', 'it must be so difficult managing your type of hair; I would hate it', 'Can I touch it? Ewww it feels weird'.

I never addressed these comments directly to the individuals or filed a complaint. Perhaps I was concerned about being called sensitive or overreactive. Instead, I decided to fight back in a different way. Rather than let these experiences crush me, I decided to let them drive my success. The times when they would head to the pub straight after school, I would create new resources and whole-school strategies. In my second year, I was promoted to assistant headteacher and achieved my Lead Practitioner accreditation. My headteacher wrote me a card that read, 'congratulations on being the first Black female assistant headteacher' in my town.

Since leaving that school, I have had leadership positions in schools of varying contexts. Some have provided similar experiences. Ultimately, I have come to accept that being a senior leader as a Black woman can be lonely at the top.

Genevieve Bent – Finding your feet as a Black woman in leadership

Genevieve Bent is an associate vice principal, overseeing Post 16, Assessment & Reporting, and Initial Teacher Training. She is a former head of science and assistant principal, an experienced A-Level Chemistry teacher, and has a Master's in science education from Kings College London. She has worked with several organisations in an educational capacity, particularly in and around STEM education and Black British history; from ITV, TES and Oxford University Press, to the British Science Association, and more.

As I celebrate the milestone of 10 years in teaching, it is one that I did not believe I would reach. I started my career in inner-city, southeast London, just down the road from where I attended school myself, and after a fantastic PGCE year, where I received strong feedback and discussed NQT roles for the coming year, I was looking forward to starting somewhere new and shiny.

I learned quickly that there would be many students who looked like me in these inner-city schools, but that would not be reflected in the workforce. I was one of just a few teaching staff who were Black, which dwindled to just one in a brief period … me.

Being a Black woman (person) in Education, certainly in my first couple of years of teaching, was lonely, at times isolating, and often demotivating. I had some lovely colleagues, one of whom started with me (as newly qualified teachers) – we had lots in common and got on very well (to this day we are friends), but she left teaching about 18 months in, and this left a big gap in my day-to-day work life. My head of department (who joined the year after I did) was a white man, and we had little in common; I did not feel empowered, valued or 'good at my job'.

As a Black woman in the working world, many of us will know what it means to code switch – the 'process of shifting from one linguistic code (a language or dialect) to another, depending on the social context or conversational setting … particularly by members of minority ethnic groups' (Morrison, 2022). We will also know what it means to not show up as our authentic selves each day, to avoid being stereotyped as 'aggressive' or 'angry' or 'over-ambitious', and therefore become mentally and physically drained from the show we (feel pressured to) put on each day. Add to that the workload and external factors in the teaching profession, and the day job can become truly exhausting. So much so that towards the end of my NQT year, I had no choice but to move to part-time because of my health.

Additionally, as a woman in education, we know that we far outweigh our male counterparts in the workforce: 'School teaching has long been associated with women. There has been an ideological link between women's domestic role and their career as schoolteacher' (Ullah, 2016).

Despite this, at senior levels, there is what feels like an overwhelming majority of men; from executive headteachers, through to assistant heads; leadership teams often seem very male dominated. In April 2022, the Department for Education (DfE) published a report titled 'School leadership in England 2010 to 2020: characteristics and trends', which showed that though there had been an increase in female leaders across both the primary and secondary phases, men progressed faster: 'in 2020, the median male teacher new to a leadership position in primary schools had been qualified for 8 years or less, compared with 10 years or less, for the median female teacher' (DfE, 2022). During my first two years in teaching, I was led by an exclusively male senior leadership team. I found it hard to see my future progression in teaching and would therefore need to focus on making as much of a difference as I could, within the realms of my classroom.

In my fourth year of teaching, I was fortunate enough to be part of a school which would now be led by one of the few Black female headteachers in the country. She was truly the first leader I had come across that not only saw my potential but gave me the opportunities to fulfil it. She was a leader to aspire to, and someone who gave me the time and support to develop, as a new middle leader (head of science).

Fast forward a few years, I am now an associate vice principal who is not only a confident practitioner, but also a member of the senior leadership team affecting whole-school change – responsible for everything Key Stage 5, alongside Initial Teacher Training routes, and Assessment, Recording and Reporting. Though I am *still* exhausted (an occupational hazard!), I am a happy and effective leader who believes wholeheartedly in my capacity to lead. My passion for education has led to this Black woman being on national TV, writing in the *Times Educational Supplement*, and collaborating with several institutions outside of my day job.

I completed a Master's degree with a thesis centred on the research and reflections of Black girls in the (science) classroom, which detailed their historic marginalisation in education and in STEM; experiences which often parallel the 'Black female teacher experience'.

Teaching is an intense (and often criticised) profession, and there is (what is commonly referred to as) a five-year itch. The effort and (what sometimes feels like) relentlessness required in teaching cause many to join and then leave, and the teacher shortage often gets worse each year. But as a Black woman in education, an already marginalised group in society historically, this can sometimes feel as if it might be just too many sacrifices – so what is my advice?

Find your tribe. After two years, I was ready to leave; my family told me to try somewhere else, and my close friend and colleague at the time, pushed me to do the same. Today, I work with some of the most amazing colleagues, and even best friends, I could not have imagined. Your wellbeing is more important than anything else; no one should feel alone in the workplace, so find somewhere you feel valued and valuable. I have also been in the fortunate position of mentoring or line-managing Black women like me and know how lucky I am to be in this position.

As a woman, there is no doubt that you will be joining a profession with a hierarchy, traditionally, of women at the 'bottom' and men at the top. Being a classroom teacher is enough – there is no doubt about that. But should you want to move up the ranks, and into leadership, **maintain tunnel vision**. Take on opportunities, network and get to know people (education is a small world), and do not *solely* rely on your great work to do the talking – as described earlier, men spend a shorter time in the profession before soaring to middle and senior leadership. **Go for what you want** and if you do not, or cannot, get it where you are, **do not be afraid to pursue it elsewhere**.

Lastly, there will be other Black women just like myself; those who are finding their feet, unsure of their position; or those who aspire to do more and work their way into positions of leadership but do not know how. Whilst making your way up, **look back down to assist those below in making their journey** – whether that's just advice, information, a point in the right direction, or more.

References

Department for Education (DfE) (2022) *School Leadership in England 2010 to 2020: Characteristics and Trends*. London: DfE.

Morrison, C.D. (2022, September 18) *Code-Switching*. Retrieved from Brittanica: www.britannica.com/topic/code-switching.

Ullah, H. (2016) School teaching as a feminine profession: The legitimization and naturalization discourses in Pakistani context. *Papers from the Education Doctoral Research Conference* (pp. 122–130). Birmingham, November.

Big questions

- Who do you aspire to be?
- What is your why? What is your purpose?
- Do you show up as your authentic self each day? If not, what can you change to be able to do so?

7

Effective Networking

Kemi – Make it work

There is power in effective networking and making meaningful connections that can be beneficial for all involved. Sometimes people want to help and support you and they ask for nothing in return. It's important to keep networking and to follow up on connections made because the older I've gotten, the more I understand it's not just what you know, but who you know and who you align, associate and connect with that can change the trajectory of your life, career and business. I remember being told that the job promotions and career opportunities happen outside of the classroom, specifically the pub or staff socials. I wasn't always interested in attending these events earlier in my career, but once I had that statement in my head, I made more of an effort. I got to know colleagues and those in positions I wanted to be in on a different level and I was able to learn from some people.

I've been fortunate enough to work with inspirational people over the course of my career and the majority of them I met when I started YBTN. This has allowed me to broaden my horizons, think bigger and to also be challenged by going for what I want and where I see myself in the future. Networking has kept me on my toes and being a forward thinker. I also make an effort to network with people who aren't in the education sector and to step outside of the education box to broaden my horizons. There's a lot you can learn from someone who is in a different industry from you and things you can apply to your situation that will be helpful. I go to a variety of events and enjoy meeting people face to face. Issa Rae said it best when she spoke about Horizontal Networking. It's not always about who's above you, but also who is beside you, so you can help each other build and grow. I'm also not ashamed of reaching out to people on social media and it has worked for my career. The worst a person can say is 'no' or not reply and even if that's the case, it's not the end of the world. Keep it moving.

I've been blessed with various opportunities to collaborate with different people and companies and I've also been able to bless others. When I started YBTN, I made it clear that I didn't have all the answers, and I'm not supposed to, otherwise there would be no room for growth. However, I always make it clear that if I cannot help directly, I will try to point them in the right direction or connect them to somebody who can.

Not all connections will be beneficial to you right away, but they could come in handy down the line. Not all connections are for you either; they could be meant for someone else that you'll meet one day and you are the link. Some amazing friendships have also blossomed from networking over the years and I believe God placed those people in my life for a reason. The YBTN team are people who saw what I was trying to do and bought into my vision for Black educators; our values align and we share a common goal which makes working together smooth and seamless.

I've had people with many years of experience in education mentor me and coach me; they've held me accountable and forced me to think outside of the box I placed myself in, and I don't believe that would've ever happened unless I networked effectively, made meaningful connections and then followed up on those connections. Remember, human beings meet a lot of other people every day, so it's important that you make a good first impression as well as ensure you follow up so you're remembered.

Caren – The interplay of networking and nepotism in teachers' career development

In the highly competitive field of early career educational recruitment, the path to securing a teaching position often extends beyond the traditional measures of qualifications and experience.

Networking is the strategic cultivation of professional relationships, whilst nepotism is the practice of favouritism towards relatives or friends – both exert a notable influence on teachers' career trajectory. It might be distasteful to admit it, but I know that my career and those of many of my friends have been rescued by these practices. Is it ethical to 'call a friend'? Is it fair? Or is that just the way the world works, and ignoring these informal channels could lead to career suicide?

Networking offers a multitude of advantages to teachers throughout their career. A robust professional network grants access to a 'hidden job market' where positions are disseminated through informal channels (Nathan, 2012). Furthermore, networks provide teachers with mentorship opportunities, insights into best practices, and support structures that bolster career growth and resilience (Baker-Doyle, 2010). Conferences, professional associations and social media platforms dedicated to educators, facilitate the expansion and maintenance of these often crucial networks.

Nepotism, while often deemed an unethical practice, remains a prevalent reality in the educational hiring process. Teachers with familial or social connections within school systems may enjoy preferential treatment, potentially bypassing more qualified candidates (DiMartino and Jessen, 2018). Such practices erode the validity of merit-based systems and undermine the perceived legitimacy of hiring decisions. Let's all be honest – how many times have you seen someone show up for an interview and you knew from their connections to other staff in the school, the job was theirs? It's an annual occurrence.

The tension between networking and nepotism highlights the complex interplay of social capital and meritocracy in teaching careers. We hammer home to students that they need to increase their social capital, but we rarely tell them the unspoken rule: you need to be a desirable hire first.

Ideally, all (teaching) positions should be awarded based on an individual's pedagogical skills, qualifications and relevant experience. However, the power of personal connections undeniably shapes opportunities within teaching (Bourdieu, 1986). When a candidate knows the school, understands the ethos, can manage the students and has been rubber-stamped with the approval of another staff member, it seems like a no brainer to hire them. This can be particularly demotivating for early-career teachers without pre-established networks or connections.

Therefore, it's crucial that these ECTs invest in networking from the start of their career, if not before. It remains an essential career development tool. Its benefits include:

- Exposure to unlisted opportunities: networking alerts teachers to job openings that might not yet be publicly advertised (Nathan, 2012).
- Mentorship and professional enhancement: experienced educators within a network offer guidance, support professional development and share innovative teaching strategies/resources.
- Career resilience: a strong network provides emotional support and resources for navigating career challenges and transitions.

To mitigate nepotism's negative impact and promote equitable hiring, educational institutions must also prioritise:

- Transparency and accountability: clear job descriptions, well-defined selection criteria and diverse interview panels, which can reduce bias and increase transparency (DiMartino and Jessen, 2018).

- Merit-focused recognition: emphasising teacher performance and contributions over personal connections promotes a culture of meritocracy and encourages unlikely candidates to apply.
- Blind hiring practices: anonymising applications can minimise unconscious bias related to names, connections or demographics.

Whilst many of these recommendations are already common practice in most schools, it's important to recognise that networking and nepotism can co-exist. Teachers should leverage networking for career growth, while advocating for transparent systems that uphold meritocracy. By nurturing genuine connections, highlighting their skills and demonstrating professionalism, teachers increase their chances of finding high-quality and fulfilling positions as they progress within their careers.

References

Baker-Doyle, K. (2010) The social side of learning: Networks and professional learning. *School Library Monthly*, 27 (2), 22–24.

Bourdieu, P. (1986) The forms of capital. In J. Richardson (ed.), *Handbook of Theory and Research for the Sociology of Education* (pp. 241–258). Westport, CT: Greenwood.

DiMartino, C. and Jessen, S.B. (2018) Nepotism in the hiring process and its consequences. *The IUP Journal of Governance and Public Policy*, XIII (2), 7–26.

Nathan, H. (2012) *How to Land a Top-Paying High School English Teacher's Job: Your Complete Guide to Opportunities, Resumes and Cover Letters, Interviews, Salaries, Promotions, What to Expect from Recruiters and More* [Ebook]. Brisbane, Australia: Emereo Publishing.

Albert Adeyemi – Black Men Teach: Unlocking a realm of connections, aspiration and opportunity through effective networking

Albert Adeyemi has been a qualified teacher for over five years. He teaches PE and Maths as well as being a head of year. Albert is also co-founder of Black Men Teach, an education network raising the profile of Black men in education.

Growing up, I was naïve to the challenges Black educators could face within the education system, as during my own schooling throughout secondary and sixth form I experienced a wealth of ethnically diverse teachers and senior leaders, including a Black female headteacher. It wasn't until I attended university where I was the only Black person on my cohort training to become a physical education teacher, that I realised the significance of having a network of support – a community who understood my background, culture and the challenges I may experience, and able to provide the guidance required to navigate not only through the education space successfully but also life in its entirety. As much as I enjoyed my time at university, I was isolated and honestly didn't have anyone I felt comfortable enough to turn to who I thought would understand me. Unbeknowst to me, there was a wider world of educators readily available and willing to impart advice, support and guidance. There were education networks out there providing support to educators from 'Black and Minority Ethnic' groups. It wasn't until 2017 (my final year at university) that I unlocked the potential of Twitter, where I discovered this community of educators of varying backgrounds, ethnicities and experiences, educators from all over the UK and indeed the world. In hindsight, subconsciously I was probably searching for a sense of belonging. My ongoing journey through education led me to co-found Black Men Teach (BMT) with Johnoi Josephs, an education network leading the way to raising the profile of Black men in education. As the data shows, the teacher workforce is a predominantly white space, so it is easy for Black or other ethnically diverse educators to feel like an anomaly, as Jeffrey Boakye describes in his book *I Heard What You Said* (2022). It's easy for non-white educators to feel like they don't belong, especially in parts of the UK, or the world, that are less diverse.

Networking can be quite a daunting task, especially for those new to teaching and those who are unfamiliar with social media. Individuals may also question the reception they will receive online, if any at all; however, it's crucial to not let these act as a barrier to accessing the greatness that social media has to offer, from teaching resources to your next career move. Personally, I just began to put myself out there. What does that even mean? I hear you say. Well, I began following various accounts on Twitter particularly, but also on LinkedIn, that aligned with my interests and my role in school but also my aspirations. I then saw that sharing good practice and resources was commonplace, so too was requesting advice – and people actually responded. I too began sharing some of my own practice, whether it be teaching physical education or mentoring. I engaged in conversations, shared my resources and soon I was fully immersed in the world of #EduTwitter.

But how do we go beyond this? How do we begin making these connections in the 'real' world? Well, ultimately, the answer is simple; you have to seize opportunities to meet and connect face to face. Funnily enough, my first opportunity to do this was at an event for Black Men in Education, organised by

Dami Iteye-Obi (Black Men in Ed lead for YBTN) and Kemi Oloyede, the founder of Young Black Teachers Network (YBTN) and co-author of this book. I was incredibly nervous and I attended alone as at the time I didn't know any Black male educators who I could invite to attend with me. However, when I arrived and saw the various activities and speakers, I realised I was definitely not alone. It was at this event that I first encountered a Black male headteacher and also connected with an assistant headteacher and SENDCo who I am still in contact with and who has been an advocate of our work at BMT. The point being that when you step out of your comfort zone and go beyond networking online, you step into a realm of aspirations and opportunities.

Many of the most significant connections I've made within the world of education have stemmed from Twitter. They have influenced my practice and career aspirations, and provided opportunities for me to collaborate with some amazing educators and organisations – in my short time in education, I have managed to achieve things I could never have imagined back when I was a trainee at university. One of my most notable achievements being co-founding Black Men Teach alongside Johnoi, who I first connected with on Twitter due to our shared passion for mentoring. We all know that when you become a teacher you're signing up for a life of service, but we decided to double down and extend this beyond our roles in our respective schools. Johnoi describes effective networking as 'relinquishing the desired narrative to be the "one and only" and the mindset of "what can I get from you?" for a group identity. The narrative becomes "we are" and "how can I support you?"'. Through BMT, we aim to provide Black male educators with a safe space where they can access the support they require, a place where they can connect with others, be inspired, discover new further opportunities – all led by Black men who understand, care and are willing to support.

Being the leaders of a growing community, we now have to consider how we network, not only for ourselves, but also for our organisation in order for us to positively impact our stakeholders. The effectiveness of our networking can determine the longevity and success of our organisation altogether. *But how do we measure this success, and how do we ensure networking is done effectively?* We developed a networking strategy, which began with our vision. What did we want to achieve for our community of educators, how were we going to do this, who could help us with particular aspects, and so on? When I say strategy, there was no big masterplan, there were no intense strategic meetings; in fact, we've never actually called it a strategy until now. Our strategy developed itself authentically through having a vision of what we wanted to achieve, connecting with experienced educators and having conversations regarding what rooms or spaces we need to be in to achieve it. Following vision came visibility. For a network, visibility is everything, both for the people you aim to serve and for anyone who might add value to your community, whether that be financially or through a service they could offer your stakeholders. Just like most networks, we have to connect with a range of speakers, venue providers, sponsors and the list goes on. *How did we go about becoming visible in the education space?* We attended events, reached out to people for opportunities, requested help, shared our vision and what we do literally everywhere we went – when you're so passionate about something, you never get bored of sharing it with people.

Key points to take away:

- Don't be afraid to step out of your comfort zone and into the world of #EduTwitter – remember, you can always utilise the block button for any negative vibes.
- Discover your vision or reason for networking – what do you want to achieve? This will help you be more intentional with your networking and align with individuals/organisations who have a shared vision.
- Take your connections beyond Twitter into the real world, go to in-person events, be visible and put yourself out there.
- Finally, think not only about what you need but what you have to offer. You know what they say, iron sharpens iron – so how can you add value to someone else?

Reference

Boakye, J. (2022) *I Heard What You Said*. London: Pan Macmillan.

Michaela Watson – A Black teacher's survival depends on their network

Michaela Lawson is the founder of Building Anti Racist Education (formerly The Prosperity Project), an organisation dedicated to advancing the racial literacy of all in schools across the UK and beyond. Michaela was formerly a primary school teacher and uses her knowledge of education to implement bespoke anti-racism training in different contexts.

'Without my Black teacher and my other Black friends, I would not survive here.'

For Black teachers and students, an effective network is essential for survival. This was actually one of the driving forces for me deciding to train as a teacher in the first place. Growing up in Berkshire, in a predominantly white area where only three of us in the year were Black and two of those mixed race, at school we had no one to vouch for us. This was true despite having one Black teacher. The expectation that she'd be on our side was short-lived, and I learned that the mere existence of more Black people does not equal community. We were lost.

Ultimately, the reasons for why I joined the profession became among the reasons why I left in 2021. Being faced with constant microaggressions and comments about my appearance; having to code switch every day; feeling like I had to 'represent my race'; being relied upon for curriculum content relating to anything 'Black'; all of this was exhausting and the list goes on. This feeling of isolation mirrored my experiences as a student. Something had to change.

The problem was therefore a lack of community that could be leveraged to change the racism we experienced. So, I founded BARE (Building Anti Racist Education) to create anti-racist cultures in schools across England, powered by our findings from focus groups with Black students and staff. In this vein, the success of my organisation lies entirely in the community we build and hold space for. These 'mini networks' inspire students and staff alike to create their own affinity groups and communities, and we can connect them with others.

I was recently invited to a student-led fashion show at a large secondary girls' school in south-east London, one of the schools in our network. The school had reframed their art and design curriculum following our programme. They went further than simply inviting the girls to design clothes incorporating their cultures, but also invited critical thinking about how fashion has been used as a statement through time, about unequal access to clothing and other broad topics. This led one of the students to design a gorgeous dress with problematic statements that Trump had made over the years, which was absolutely hilarious. What was so significant about this event though was the community that had been created as a result. The students themselves sought out peers who would be make-up artists, designers, models, and even curate the music for the day. Their relationships with teachers they previously didn't engage with built and improved, and ultimately they created an effective network out of a shared love of fashion.

And that is what is important. A network does not have to be a stuffy, transactional, corporate relationship or exclusive club that the Western capitalist lens would have us believe. You only have to think about a networking event, and a group of middle-aged white men in blue shirts likely comes to mind. Individualism does not serve us, but in fact actively upholds the structures that oppress us. Our very survival as Black people, in the face of systematic racism, has been dependent on our communities. As the African proverb goes, 'it takes a village to raise a child'.

Effective networking is about creating intentional community, through shared experiences. You cannot understate the community you can build just through facilitating conversation, sharing a space with people who share a common inter-est. Before I was a teacher, I would hold philosophical symposiums as a hobby, not knowing that the people that I'd meet there would include one of my first trainers and my website copywriter. You already have a community. Start there:

1   What are you trying to get out of a network or community?
2   Why is this important to you?
3   What shared experience will ground you in this connection?

Daniel Robinson – Helping teachers to link up

Daniel Robinson is an assistant headteacher serving young people from an inner London community. Daniel has used his professional experience, love for others and a can-do attitude to create networking events uniquely designed to support Black teachers, meet peers and party hard!

Lonely! This is the word I would use to describe my first three years as a teacher. Having grown up in a large town just outside of London, completing my degree in Birmingham, training to be a teacher in Manchester and beginning my ECT journey in London – I was very familiar with meeting new people and making new friends. But nothing prepared me for the vulnerabilities that I felt moving between classrooms, as the responsible adult, who was in some cases only five years older than some of the 'children' I was serving! What confounded my newly felt sense of exposure was the lack of connection I had with my new colleagues. I felt so foreign in the staffroom, cut out of CPD conversations, and I shared so few cultural references, that I sometimes felt like a Jamaican mongoose, hovering around English squirrels. In short, I was out of place in every part of the building and had to make my car rides to and from school, listening to Sway and Drake, my temporary sanctuary.

This anxious daily belly churning led me to the realisation that schools really are very middle-class and white spaces, where I and other Black or working-class teachers felt out of place. But I was determined to change this and provide teach-ers with similar experiences to mine, an opportunity to socialise, to realise that we can be unashamedly Black within our profession and meet Black colleagues in a wide range of positions, showing that Black people matter to our profession and the young people we serve.

In 2016, I gained a promotion and changed school, moving to a more diverse borough in east London, and which had a more diverse staff body, but the dominant white habitus still ran through the school and meant the only way to socialise was through drinking at the pub. So what could these networking hubs look like? What would best celebrate Black teachers' similarities? What would show the identity of a Black teacher best? This was a conversation I had with a fellow Black middle leader in a rare trip to a pub one Friday afternoon, while observing a colleague down her sixth pint of Guinness! And this conversation served as our first discussion about what would become TeacherLinkup.

Like so many great ideas relating to education, TeacherLinkup didn't actually come into fruition until 2018. TeacherLinkup's co-founder received a promotion and moved to a new school down south, increasing our network and confounding our feelings that London's education system needed this idea. Towards the end of 2017, we decided – we'd be doing party nights!

We pushed forward as a group of three, with the co-founder mentioned above introducing a member of support staff at his school, to help us bring this vision to life. I largely became the processes person – I used my ability to get things done to research similar events in other fields such as NHS parties, and contacted potential locations in my first attempt at navigating the minefield that is putting on events for Black people. The teacher from south London naturally took the lead with music and ensuring the vibe was perfect for Black teachers. He was the main DJ but contacted his friends to ensure different aspects of the culture were represented. The newest member of TeacherLinkup worked on our visuals and took responsibility for promoting the event with me.

Our events were a hit, with us often selling out, the vibe was exciting and it was great to see like-minded people speak to each other and enjoy time away from the classroom and celebrate the diversity of our great profession. Connections were made between peers and working relations were strengthened. Through our events, ECTs met middle leaders and middle leaders met senior leaders, and we as teachers and support staff created the networks that we didn't even know were needed. This is the aspect of TeacherLinkup that I am most proud of, as we helped other out-of-place colleagues realise that the teaching profession is for us!

In 2021, I changed job again and I am now a senior leader in a different east London school. In my new position, I prioritise championing staff who come from underrepresented groups and actively look for opportunities to connect new staff as I don't want teachers to feel alone, and I use the connections made personally from TeacherLinkup to identify support, open up positive discussions and highlight issues of the Black child and the Black teacher.

Social media is the new staffroom for some colleagues but the importance of meeting in person cannot be underestimated. TeacherLinkup is not a thing of the past and we will return. We look forward to welcoming guests again and to continue what we started for a new generation of ECTs, established teachers, middle leaders, senior leaders and support staff!

Olajumoke Champion – Networking for success

Olajumoke Champion started her career as a teacher of computer science and head of year; after five years in the education industry, she changed her career path into project management. Olajumoke is dynamic and result oriented; she is highly educated with a BSc in Business Information Systems (first class), a Postgraduate Certificate in Education and Computer Science, an MSc in Strategic Management, and Prince2 Practitioner and ITIL certifications.

'Your network is your net worth' is a saying we are all familiar with, yet we undervalue the power of networking and how the potential benefits can help us develop personally and professionally. Networking can be an invaluable tool for Black ethnic minorities due to the multiple challenges we face in the workplace.

Those who understand how valuable networking is are the ones who gain the most benefits.

Some of the benefits of networking are:

- access to a hidden jobs market
- the development of high-profile contacts
- that it can help with barriers to entry
- that it offers new perspectives/creative ideas
- that it makes you noticeable
- the ability to draw on a wealth of knowledge and support.

Effective networking is a give-and-take activity and, in an already competitive market where Black ethnic minority groups often have to work twice as hard as their counterparts, it is crucial to establish strong connections and build relationships that you can draw on whilst building a career in education.

Here is how effective networking has increased my net worth.

Building meaningful relationships

Building good relationships with my managers, colleagues and industry experts landed me a promotion, additional responsibilities and three pay rises in just two years.

Whilst working in one of my previous roles, I built and nurtured strong relationships with my managers and colleagues across the school by *listening and actively participating*, and engaging with them, both formally and informally. I worked with my mentor closely for six months, shadowing and making myself available, as well as volunteering, to take on tasks that gave me exposure across the school.

In our weekly meetings, we would *document goals, talk career progression and actions to take*, with evidence detailing how I was meeting the teacher standards. This was crucial as it was a significant factor when it came to interviewing for additional responsibility and discussions regarding pay.

With cross-department networking, the consistent support from my manager and the career advice I received, I was able to get additional responsibility every year from when I joined the school until the year I left.

Lessons and applications

- Seek out mentorship as it can expose you to high-profile individuals, opportunities and advice.
- You need other people to be great – utilise the people and resources around you.
- There is something to be learned from every experience (work hard enough that you cannot be ignored).
- We can use our networks to create more opportunities and open more doors for other Black ethnic minorities.
- Never go to meetings with management underprepared.
- Use all experiences to grow your personal and professional brand.
- Try to add value to every interaction, even if the outcome seems negative, as you don't know what doors you can open.
- Barriers to entry can be reduced with the knowledge and experience you acquire.

Professional development and networking events

Continuous professional development and networking in education are essential as it's an industry that is constantly evolving and is also interdependent on a range of external agencies.

In order to boost my profile, knowledge and gain contacts that I could potentially call on in the future, I booked myself on to online training courses and attended networking conferences.

I also looked up the relevant associations to join which enabled me to further grow my knowledge and access thought leadership. These actions helped me build a network of contacts that I could draw on when I became head of year, which was useful when leading talks or organising school trips/events.

It also amplified my personal brand and LinkedIn profile which made me noticeable. When I reached the peak of progression in my current role (glass ceiling), micro-aggressive comments followed such as 'I didn't know you would have such an impact when you first came'. At that point, I knew it was time to start the daunting process of job searching.

While applying to multiple roles through LinkedIn, I had a successful screening interview, which was followed up with a call. Using *positive engagement and listening skills*, we discovered that although the job was not for me, she was so impressed with my positive attitude and assertiveness that during the conversation she said 'I'd like to help you with your CV. I don't think it will get the traction you require'. We followed up on this and she assisted me with a tailor-made, fit-for-purpose CV that garnered more attention. Once my CV was getting increased consideration and my profile was more noticeable, I was headhunted to apply for lead roles and opportunities to teach abroad. I landed a new role and received a salary increase with exceptional benefits. I still have this contact on LinkedIn, plus her personal contact number, and she has since reached out to me regarding other job opportunities.

Overcoming the lack of representation

As a minority, there is a lack of representation in educational leadership, workplaces and networking events. Being the minority in the room can be challenging as you stand out and tend to code switch to ensure that how you behave and what you have said are not interpreted negatively.

I was recently at an event where there were very few minorities, but I did not allow this to discourage me. I ensured I was well prepared for conversations and interactions by doing some initial research and *asking the right questions*.

I made a conscious effort to not be drawn only to the Black ethnic minorities, as there is a lot to learn from people of different backgrounds, and the primary focus here should be building contacts that you can draw on to support you both personally and professionally.

Lessons and applications
- Operate out of growth, not survival. Don't only be drawn to people like you; try to speak to everyone; all contacts can be useful in different avenues.
- Leaders need to ensure diversity in workplace culture and events.
- It's a privilege to be at the forefront of someone's mind when an opportunity arises.
- Show up, as representation matters in networking and workplace environments. Your presence alone can put someone else at ease.
- Networking is for both introverts and extroverts – you don't know what opportunities this can present for people around you.

- Do some research and be prepared to ask the right questions; this will help you feel more confident.
- Building yourself as a brand and being memorable will have you spoken about in rooms full of opportunities that you may not be in.
- The more people you meet, the more self-confidence you have, and the more daring you become to step outside of your comfort zone.

Be willing to engage in difficult conversations

During a weekly meeting with a colleague, the taboo subject of salary came up and I realised that my colleague was getting paid more, despite the fact that we were doing the same job and I had additional tasks (a classic example of having to work harder than our counterparts to stand out).

This experience highlighted the importance of having *uncomfortable conversations*. As a Black person in a workplace, it's important to be brave and be ready to have difficult conversations; communicating in an effective way is fundamental. I followed this conversation up with a formal email to my line manager to request a pay rise. Although I was not offered the total salary difference, I was able to close the pay gap and some of my tasks were delegated to other members of staff.

Cross-collaboration and discussions with colleagues (internal and external to the school) may give you new insights and knowledge that you can use to your advantage. This could be new teaching material or initiatives to bring into your school, which you may have the opportunity to lead and which may contribute to discussions on increasing your pay.

Lessons and applications
- Uncomfortable conversations broaden your perspective and remind you to be open to other people's opinions/perspectives.
- Be clear on how you feel and what you want the outcome to be.
- When you initiate uncomfortable conversations, you are in a better position to navigate how it will proceed.

An opportunity lost turned into an opportunity won

I was excited about applying for a middle-management role and there were two of us going for the job. I felt like I aced the interview, but I did not get the job.

Other members of staff were surprised that the other person was given the job and it became a topic at work. It was a clear representation of not getting a promotion due to workplace bias.

However, not getting the job made me seek out new experiences to boost my profile and presence. I shadowed different members of leadership who had been in the role I had applied for (all from minority ethnic groups). Connecting with people in leadership, combined with raising my profile around the organisation and involving myself in more workplace communities made me, my work and my talent *impossible to ignore*.

When the next head of year job came up, I was approached to apply for the job. Fortunately (or coincidentally), I got the job for the year group with the most Black male students. I was really able to make a difference in some of those lives.

Lessons and applications

- Put in the hard work and eventually you will be noticed to the point where your work cannot be ignored, even when bias is involved.
- Representation in leadership and middle management matters; seeing other minorities doing well allows for others to be inspired (don't be afraid to be the representation).
- It has been said that performance counts for 10% of your success, image for 30% and exposure for 60%. As a Black ethnic minority, I believe that image and performance are of equal footing but exposure can put you ahead of the game.

Rhia Gibbs – Your network really is your net worth

Rhia is a consultant with a passion for helping clients to bring about innovative and lasting change. Rhia has a passion for people, and this is reflected in her founding a global network of Black teachers – Black Teachers Connect. As a former teacher of sociology and head of Year 12, making true change is what is at the core of Rhia's work.

A fruitful and supportive network is probably the key to Black teachers surviving the classroom in the 21st century. It is often a taken-for-granted and over-simplified concept, but networking can be a key to both personal and professional development for Black teachers. In the teaching profession, your network really is your 'net worth'. It is also not as easy as it seems. When I was actively looking for support when joining the profession in late 2017, I could not find a massive network of Black teachers but was lucky enough to have known a few that could support me with my application. But it always dawned on me, what if I had never been so lucky?

Creating community

Once accepted onto my PGCE, I stood from a point of view that I never wanted any Black individual to experience this lack of network if they wanted to embark on a journey into the teaching profession, which led to me founding Black Teachers Connect in June 2018. It was an idea I had pondered over for a while, and we first began this just in a digital space via Twitter. Black Teachers Connect was one of the UK's first teacher networks solely for Black African and Black Caribbean teachers: a space truly for Black teachers to thrive and network effectively and a community where we can support and help one another to truly grow. We have gone on to support thousands of Black teachers globally, and this has meant that we have been able to bring teachers into a networking sphere where they can support, advise and mentor one another. We have since become a Community Interest Company where we continue to invest and pour into the success of Black teachers. Since founding Black Teachers Connect, many pivotal organisations like YBTN, Black Men in ED and Aspiring Heads (just to name a few) have launched and given effective networking spaces to Black teachers.

Why network?

Have any of your students ever questioned why they must work in a group or why they must work in a pair? Have you explained the importance of collaboration to that student? The answer is probably yes. In the same way that students can often forget the importance of collaboration, sometimes teachers can too. The value in having a network can often be forgotten. Some Black teachers stand in isolation as the only Black teacher in their school. This can be daunting, scary and take its toll on mental health.

   I remember times during my teaching career where I felt like I had nobody to turn to, but I had my mentor (a female Black former headteacher) or I had both Black women and men that I had managed to meet at events, through social media networks like Twitter and LinkedIn (more on this later) that I could seek advice and mentorship from. I often wonder, what would have been the result if I did not have such an extensive network? Would my vigour and passion be ignited or would I burn out? The key to my survival was my network.

The genuine support that I received was the reason why I find so much value in networking, and you should too.

Networking not only builds confidence for Black teachers, it helps them to get different perspectives and ideas for solving problems, helps career development and professional development. But something which I think is underestimated in networking is the personal growth and development you receive. As much as we are teachers, we are still human, and humans thrive on relationships. Some of my best friendships and relationships have begun from someone simply being a work colleague. Building up not only professional friends but personal friends can help support your wellbeing and mental health, two things which are often neglected in the teaching profession.

How do Black teachers network?

Teachers are often like students and need direct instruction! I have discussed a lot about the importance of networking, but I do want to give actionable tips for Black teachers who struggle to build their network in an effective way. Networking will not happen overnight, nor will it be a super easy process, but it will be worth it:

- Join a professional network which is tailored towards you and what you are looking for. That could be Black Teachers Connect or any other similar network, but this will be a good place to start connecting with like-minded individuals and teachers that can support you.
- The most useful tool that has helped develop my professional network would have to be the use of Twitter and LinkedIn. These tools are both free and so useful for building up a network. They have allowed me to connect with those who are more senior in the profession and can therefore offer me advice and mentorship. Many people often ask me how to utilise these social media sites to their full potential. The best piece of advice I can give is to be bold. Jump into direct messages and ask people for support or advice. Quite often, teachers are very supportive and happy to help one another.
- The virtual world is great but going to real, in-person events holds value. You can meet a range of individuals, especially those who do not use social media and you can have meaningful conversations and make useful connections. This means that you will have to actively look for opportunities to network in person. Networking will only work if you are willing to invest time in it.

As you journey through your career, always look at those around you and continue to build up your network. You deserve to thrive as an educator and a key to this is building up your network.

Big questions

• How are you building your network in your career? What can you do now
  to build a great network?
• Does your school actively support teachers to network effectively?
• Has your current network been impactful or ineffective?

8

Reading Matters

Caren – The importance of continuous teacher training and development in all schools

A highly skilled and continually developing teaching workforce is essential in ensuring our students meet the educational outcomes we seek and make continued progress. Effective teacher training and continuous professional development (CPD) directly influence student achievement, teacher retention, and the overall elevation of educational standards across the country. If a workforce is well read, with regular updates on cutting-edge research and pedagogy, it can only benefit the school and their community.

Initial teacher training (ITT) forms the foundation of a teacher's career. In the UK, ITT programmes ensure that aspiring teachers possess the subject knowledge, pedagogical expertise and classroom management skills necessary to succeed. The delivery of this training can vary, alongside student engagement. If done well, trainees leave the course full of energy, zeal and confidence for the classroom. Research demonstrates a strong correlation between the quality of ITT and teachers' long-term effectiveness (Darling-Hammond et al., 2017). High-quality ITT programmes prepare teachers to manage the complexities of the classroom and address the diverse needs of learners.

The significance of teacher development extends far beyond the initial training phase. Continuous professional development (CPD) is essential for teachers to stay abreast of the latest pedagogical approaches, subject-specific advancements, and policy changes in education (DfE, 2016). Effective CPD programmes promote reflective practice among teachers, empowering them to identify their individual needs and pursue targeted development opportunities. A robust CPD infrastructure ensures that teachers continue to develop their skills throughout their career, enhancing their ability to support students' learning effectively.

The benefits of investing in teacher training and development are multifaceted and limitless. Studies indicate that high-quality CPD leads to improved student outcomes, particularly in core subjects like mathematics and literacy (Kraft et al., 2018). Additionally, when teachers feel invested in and supported in their professional growth, they demonstrate higher levels of job satisfaction and are more likely to remain in the profession (Darling-Hammond, 2000).

Despite the recognised significance of CPD, many schools in the UK face challenges in ensuring consistent access and quality. Ofsted's 2023 report highlights that workload pressures and a lack of dedicated funding can hinder teachers' participation in CPD activities. To address this, it is crucial to prioritise time and resources for professional development within school budgets and timetables. Additionally, providing a range of CPD formats, such as online modules or peer observations, can offer flexibility to teachers.

Furthermore, aligning CPD with school priorities ensures that development opportunities directly address the specific needs of teachers and their schools. A culture of collaboration where teachers share best practices and learn from one another is also invaluable (Ambition Institute, n.d.).

As mentioned in previous chapters, I was very lucky in my first few years of teaching to be fully supported in my training. I worked in environments where teacher development was seen as synergistic with student development. It's important to be autonomous and keep an eye out for courses, development opportunities and programmes that will both benefit your own CPD and align with school priorities. Unfortunately, it's also important to advocate for yourself and ensure that you aren't held back in any way. I have experienced both extremes and the latter is not fun at all! I actually had a headteacher call me on my way to a training session to tell me I wasn't 'allowed' to attend the free training, due to a lack of cover. I was so shell-shocked at the time, I didn't know how to respond. To this day, I don't know if I would have had the right words that would have been polite to utter.

In conclusion, prioritising teacher training and development is paramount for any school's success. Well-prepared and continuously supported teachers are better equipped to nurture student growth, foster a love of learning and raise educational standards nationwide. They are also better informed and equipped to deal with the challenges of the students and families they serve. Ongoing investment in the professional development of teachers yields far-reaching dividends, benefiting generations of students and society as a whole.

References

Ambition Institute (n.d.) *Five practical tips for effective teacher development*. www.ambition.org.uk/blog/five-practical-tips-for-effective-teacher-development.

Darling-Hammond, L. (2000). Teacher quality and student achievement. *Education Policy Analysis Archives*, 8, 1.

Darling-Hammond, L., Hyler, M. and Gardner, M. (2017). *Effective teacher professional development*. Learning Policy Institute. https://learningpolicyinstitute.org/sites/default/files/product-files/Effective_Teacher_Professional_Development_REPORT.pdf

Department for Education (DfE) (2016) *Standard for teachers' professional development*. www.gov.uk/government/publications/standard-for-teachers-professional-development.

Kraft, M.A., Blazar, D. and Hogan, D. (2018) The effect of teacher coaching on instruction and achievement. *American Educational Research Journal*, 55(2), 275–314.

Ofsted (2023) *Teachers' professional development remains a work in progress*. www.gov.uk/government/news/teachers-professional-development-remains-a-work-in-progress.

Kemi – CPD: Friend or foe?

When I first started teaching, I thought continuous professional development was just another tick-box activity that teachers do, and sometimes I still feel that way. As I wasn't thinking long term at the start of my career, I did not think of finding CPD that was applicable to me and my goals or development. I like CPD to be personalised and tailored to what I want to do and where I want to go with my career. I don't want to feel like I'm wasting my time listening to someone speak on a topic or course I have no interest in. Then I started taking matters into my own hands. When I was an NQT and in the first couple of years of my teaching career, I didn't understand how some of my colleagues were having so many days off school to go on training. No one ever told me about completing CPD request forms and that there was a budget to develop teachers. I honestly had no idea. I began doing some research and this is where I thought about where I wanted my career to go if I was to stay in teaching. I started my career in education as a learning support assistant and I enjoyed working with students with special educational needs and also finding the best ways to support them on their journey of academic success. I researched CPD that aligned with my long-term goals and vision. I took part in in-house CPD sessions that the schools I worked in put in place for staff as well as what was part of my teacher training course, but 2017 was when I took my development seriously. I went on training that developed me as a science teacher, as a careers leader and as a SENCO. In the four years I worked in a PRU, I was exposed to more roles outside of teaching and I grabbed every opportunity to learn and develop so I could apply it to my role as a SENCO. I signed up to mailing lists where CPD was emailed and shared with people all over England. I also used TES and signed up to CPD they had on offer on their website. I'd complete accredited courses too as they carried a certain level of recognition and credibility in the teaching profession.

I would apply what I learnt on my training to my school setting and subject area. I also shared what I had learnt with colleagues to inform their practice and what we wanted to do as a school. This is particularly important when you are working as a team: share the knowledge you've gained to upskill your colleagues and contribute to their development, especially if you're in a position as a leader. This is where I realised that I could potentially get into Learning & Development and consulting as a School Improvement Partner.

I've kept a portfolio of my professional development over the years; I have an online copy as well as a hard copy that I've taken with me to interviews. It's my one-stop shop for my evidence-based learning and impact. When I'm asked questions about what I can bring to the table, I have my portfolio on hand. Not only is my professional development mentally stored and I can speak about it, I also have something tangible to show as well as the impact of my CPD when I'm asked for evidence. Remember to use your CPD as an opportunity to network and mingle. It's not always what you know but who you know that can help propel your career in the direction you want it to go in. I've had the pleasure to witness what YBTN has been able to do via the events we've put on:

- Teachers have been able to support others to get roles at their schools.
- Teachers have been able to start their own networks as a result of attending our events.
- Teachers have been able to link others to further CPD opportunities they were unaware of before.

Kafilat Agboola – Charting your professional development journey: Self-determination, self-direction and the power of you

Kafilat Agboola is a science teacher, a MAT Director of Professional Learning and an executive coach with over 10 years of senior and system leadership experience. She is a #WomenEd network leader and has led programmes and networks for Black teachers.

I vividly recall the moment I approached my then headteacher to seek permission for participation in an external two-year programme designed for middle leaders. How I came across this programme is hazy, but I distinctly remember that the opportunity was subsidised by our multi-academy trust's (MAT) head office. This meant that my school would not have to pay the full £1200 fee and it would be an opportunity to form closer relationships with other schools in the MAT, a strategic goal for head office at the time.

My headteacher's response was positive. I don't remember the details of the conversation beyond the condition they gave me: I would need to remain at the school during the entire two-year period and for at least a year beyond. This condition, though delivered lightly, carried a significant weight. I was commuting for 3–4 hours daily and already very committed to the school and the work I had embarked on as a middle leader with whole-school responsibility. However, this condition made me acutely aware of the financial investment the school was making in my development. I needed to stay the course and deliver on the investment.

Interestingly, I can honestly say that without that programme, the access to external coaching and the formation of close professional contacts in particular, I would not have been able to stay the course in that role at a very challenging time in my professional life. Being even more honest, I have to say that I probably only realised 60% of the potential full benefit of that programme. I was much too busy with work to attend all programme components or engage sufficiently deeply to maximise a full return on my and the school's investment. Of course, now, I realise that the balancing act, and the prioritisation of my learning, development and building new contacts *was* the work; 14 years of people development, school and system leadership later, juggling two Master's level qualifications, an extremely busy work schedule and observing common challenges through facilitating leadership development programmes for over 500 school leaders in the last three years, I'm here to tell you, this remains the work.

It's abundantly clear to me now that this investment transcends the mere financial contribution. It can (be received to) signify the organisation's commitment to and affirmation of the individual's personal and professional growth and the value they place on their most important resource, their people. When such requests aren't granted, the individual often (understandably) feels unvalued, and their hopes or goals invalidated. However, successful requests might just be down to a clearer alignment between the individual's and organisation's goals; or even, down to luck, good timing, effective positioning or communication.

So, what about you? Can you think of a professional development activity that was notable for its impact, or lack of, on you? How are you defining impact and which time frame are you using? Keep reflecting with a spirit of curiosity. Was there anything about the professional development activity's content or design that led to that outcome? To what extent was this outcome mediated by your personal or professional context at the time? What might you take from this example (and others) to inform the next step of your professional development journey?

Connecting the personal and professional: Understanding your internal drivers

There are lots of terms associated with the learning and development of teachers and leaders, highlighting the complexity of this field. I use the terms CPD and professional development interchangeably, noting that both terms assume different meanings in different contexts. For our purposes, I define professional development as a flexible, structured and sustained set of activities, formal and informal learning opportunities that may be facilitated or self-directed, with the intention of enhancing teachers' and leaders' knowledge, skills and capacity to achieve success, however they define it.

Cultivating a learning orientation, or mindset, connects your personal and professional 'work' or development, increasing the likelihood of forward momentum in both. 'Educators must be knowledgeable and wise. They must know enough in order to change. They must change in order to get different results. They must become learners' (Easton, 2008: 756, cited by Stoll et al., 2012).

Let's learn more about your motivations and goals as this is the starting point for your self-directed learning and development journey.

If you are reading this chapter, it is likely that you are already highly motivated to pursue CPD or professional development. Let us begin by establishing clarity on your 'why'. This will be your guiding light, enabling you to focus and choose effectively during times of plenty and to stay motivated during darker times. An Ethiopian proverb I often return to is relevant here: 'anticipate the good so that you may enjoy it'. What does 'success' look like to you? What does it feel, sound, smell, look like? Once you are super clear on your goal or destination and the personal and professional significance of this for you, you will be able to look out for and celebrate the checkpoints. You'll also know if, when and how you need to adjust course to get there.

Boyatzis' (and Oosten, 2002) model of self-directed learning connects your personal and professional learning and development. A series of five non-linear steps guides you towards authenticity, mastery and the realisation of your 'ideal self'. Steps 1 and 2 are relevant here, requiring you to consider your:

1 'Ideal Self' (Who do you want to be? What do you want out of life and work?)
2 'Real Self' (How do you act? What are your strengths? Where are the gaps between your ideal and real selves?)

It may be that you want to undertake some CPD or professional development for one or more of these reasons:

- You've had feedback that there's an area of practice you need to refine or develop further. What's the evidence for this? What are the opportunities to address this in your current role or with stretch assignments?
- You want to prepare for/develop into a different role and are aware of gaps. What are the gaps and how have you diagnosed them? What are the strengths that you can leverage? Who could you run this by for objective feedback?
- You feel that you have mastered your current role/deliverables and want to be stretched/challenged. Towards what? What would others say?
- You feel frustrated or stalled in your career development. You feel that you should be further along already. What or who are you benchmarking yourself against? How valid is this?
- You are curious about another role/functional area or are generally committed to ongoing learning. What low-cost, informal opportunities are available to you in your current role?

For each answer, ask yourself new questions, go deeper and dig into your underlying motivations. Be curious about their origins. Are they intrinsic (driven by internal desires) or extrinsic (driven by external factors)? Be circumspect about how much you allow extrinsic motivators to influence your learning and development agenda, as whilst they can motivate you towards success, they are less likely to lead to growth or fulfilment. When you have settled on your 'why', be resourceful, proactive and deliberate about self-directing your learning and development. You are aiming for the 'sweet' spot between your personal, your professional and the organisation's priorities.

Connecting the personal and professional: Understanding your external context

Now you've interrogated your goals and motivations, you need to zoom out and consider how far and in which way the external context of your school can enable your professional development goals. Research on the impact of the working environment on teacher development is limited, however a culture of open and honest communication, mutual respect and enthusiasm, high levels of senior leader support to maintain classroom safety and behaviour, and opportunities for teacher collaboration, are among the aspects most closely linked to teacher development having a positive impact on student attainment (Weston et al., 2021).

You will intuitively know that school leadership's support for professional development is also essential. This is borne out by several studies (DfE, 2016;

EEF, 2021) and can be considered via two lenses. First, to what extent are school leaders aware of and supportive of your aspirations and goals? An obvious starting point is routine line management and organisation-wide people-development practices and processes such as appraisal/performance management. Read the policies and engage with the process fully, ensuring thorough preparation by your department and robust documentation on your line manager/appraiser's part. I'm under no illusion that this is a foolproof process. Elsewhere in this volume, you will no doubt be introduced to a key concept in critical race theory: 'interest convergence theory'. This is the idea that long overdue changes in society only occur for racialised or minoritised groups when they converge with the interests of the majority group. There is a direct link here: people and institutions are more likely to support you when your goals, your 'requests', align with what they want and need.

The second lens you can apply to your context, is the level of commitment to change to address the disproportionate development and progression of Black teachers. Miller (2016) proposes that there are four categories of educational institutions, determined by the progression of BME staff. Is your school 'engaged', with BME staff represented at all levels of the staffing hierarchy including leadership? Is it 'uninitiated' with no BME staff and no plan to address its legal duty or is it somewhere in between, 'experimenting' or 'initiated'?

Reflecting upon these considerations and more will help you decide your approach and tactics.

Preparing for success: Defining impact

Although intended for people such as me who have responsibility for designing, implementing and evaluating professional development in schools, consideration of Guskey's (2000) five hierarchical levels of professional development evaluation could be instructive to you as you begin with the end in mind, preparing for success, determining how you might measure impact and develop a business case:

1   **Participant reaction** – did you enjoy it? Did you think it was time well spent?
2   **Participant learning** – did you acquire the intended knowledge or skills? Were any of your beliefs or attitudes challenged or changed?
3   **Organisational (phase, department, school) support and change** – did your learning and development impact the wider organisation? Did you get sufficient support and were any challenges addressed in a timely manner?
4   **Participant use of new knowledge** – to what extent have you used your new knowledge or skills?

5 **Student learning outcomes** – have your learning and development affected *student* learning or development? Have they influenced student beliefs or attitudes? Quantitative measures of student achievement and performance are relevant but not the only measure.

There is consensus that any professional development should begin with a clear specification of the student learning outcomes to be achieved and the best data to reflect these outcomes (Guskey, 2000). The bottom line is that if it's not going to affect student outcomes in some way, at some point, the professional development is not worth doing. This may feel too narrow for you, however I'd counter that any thinking about the purpose of your professional development can be linked to student impact, if only indirectly. For example, although I'm no longer in a full-time, direct teaching role, one of the reasons I'm undertaking an MBA in educational leadership is to improve the strategic leadership and operational capacity of my organisation to deliver the best outcomes (in the broadest sense) for the students in our care. Further, a clear articulation of the expected impact on student outcomes is essential in preparing a business case, if needed, to request time off or financial contributions towards your intended professional development activity.

Shaping your learning and development agenda

Once the intended impact is clear, you can move to steps 3 and 4 in Boyatzis' model (Boyatzis and Oosten, 2002):

1 **Determine the learning agenda** (building on your strengths whilst reducing gaps)
2 **Plan for experimentation and practice** (to develop mastery with new behaviours).

Important considerations include:

Logistics: Evaluate the feasibility of engaging in professional development. Consider accessibility, location, timing. Ensure it aligns with your personal and professional commitments.

Investment: Consider the financial and time investments required for professional development. What is the true cost? Assess whether these align with your personal and professional goals and if you are able and willing to pay.

Prepare for trade-offs. You can do everything you need and want, just not at the same time. You may need to identify good things you (temporarily) stop doing in order to create time and space for better, more impactful things.

These considerations will influence the forms and approaches to professional development that you decide are best suited to your needs.

The CPD marketplace is so saturated that in many ways the challenge for you is curating your own pathway and deciding what **not** to engage with. External and internal development options include:

Online learning: The digital age offers a plethora of online courses, webinars and resources. These can be pursued at your convenience and are often cost-effective, if not free. Examples include Seneca Learning, Futurelearn, Udemy, and the National College.

Blogs, journals, newsletters, books, podcasts: An obvious and rich source of learning that is frequently overwhelming in the amount of content that is available, so be selective about what you subscribe to and what you consume. Publications such as *Schools Week* and platforms such as Teacher Tapp have helpful summaries of the latest educational books and research.

Networks and social media: Again, there are too many to list here, but it is possible to find a network or social media group for nearly every type of role. There are also several affinity networks (networks whose members share specific interests or characteristics) that you'll benefit from, some of them able to offer fully funded development programmes for Black teachers due to DfE funding.

Inquiry and research: At the smallest scale, you adopt an inquiry approach to your daily work, identifying questions worthy of exploration, reflecting on what the naturally occurring data tells you. You could scale up to significant research projects.

Developing a writing practice: Engaging in a sustained reflective writing practice develops your insights, provides space for sense making and can reconnect you to your purpose. It can even develop outstanding leadership skills (Adler, 2016). Whether you choose to keep a journal, blog or learning log, be disciplined in writing regularly and benefit from increased clarity and understanding about the world and your development.

Formal and accredited courses and programmes: These require the greatest investment of time and money so a cost-benefit analysis is essential. Programme components are likely to include all the above options with the addition of social support and peer learning. These programmes can lead to informal or professional networks that confer 'marks of affiliation', that support the progression of Black teachers (Miller, 2020). Teacher recruitment and retention challenges mean that you can currently access fully funded CPD opportunities such as National Professional Qualifications and subject-specific CPD led by curriculum hubs. It's also worth exploring apprenticeship levy funded programmes. These enable you to enrol as an apprentice and pursue wide-ranging accredited programmes at no additional cost to your employer.

Once you've designed your learning agenda, ensure it includes sufficient experiential learning where you 'learn by doing' and reflecting on the experience. Don't forget to factor in your current school's context so that your plans for professional development don't get derailed by reality.

Optimising for success: Mapping your network

At the heart of Boyatzis' model of self-directed learning is the development of trusted relationships with coaches or mentors that will support you at every step. Whatever your goal, mapping your professional learning network is a great place to start identifying where these relationships could be. Essentially, you get a piece of paper and map out all of the people and networks that you linked to that might support you on your journey. There's a couple of ways you could do this. You could consider the proximity and strength of the relationship, perhaps using concentric circles of widening radius. So, in the inner circle you might put close colleagues that you interact with on a daily or weekly basis. Then in a slightly wider circle, perhaps place mentors or senior leaders and in another, wider circle, more distant professional contacts such as teacher training course leaders or networks that you only interact with occasionally. Another approach could be to identify specific domains or foci of skill and knowledge development and map out who can help with each of them. For example, you might want to deepen your curriculum design and implementation knowledge, and you identify that subject leaders, at middle or senior level in your current school or connected schools, could help. What about those organisations that are mandated to help through the receipt of public and/or private funding? Schools designated by the Department of Education as research or curriculum hubs, unions and commercial CPD providers fall into this category. Also consider those organisations whose very mission is aligned with this area. Subject associations, researchED and the Chartered College of Teaching fall into this category. Don't neglect the innumerable authors, bloggers and researchers that produce material of varying levels of scholarship.

Here's another Ethiopian proverb for you: 'an overly modest [wo]man goes hungry'. Now you've mapped out your network, you need to access the resource and support within it. I know it is frequently difficult to put yourself out there, but you need to. This is easier once you've developed strong, mutually beneficial relationships. Look at your network map. Are there any people or networks that you'd benefit from developing a closer or deeper relationship with? What might that look like in terms of frequency, form or quality of the interactions? Have you got a mentor, coach *and* a sponsor? A sponsor is someone that uses their position and influence to advocate for you and your strengths and talents. What will it take for you to be honest and open about where you're at, what you want and what you need for your professional development? Radcliffe (2012) advises that leaders need to consciously practise building 'Big Relationships' – that is, relationships that are big enough to get the job done. Whether or not you have the official title of leader, you *are* the leader of your professional development journey. Look again at your network map. Hopefully, your line manager is on this map as well as the person that is ultimately responsible for professional development in your organisation. Is your relationship with them big enough?

Whoever you decide to foster trusted relationships with, draw upon their support to deepen your experiential learning by asking them to provide affirmation and reinforcement after progress, thereby bolstering your motivation, feedback and social support as you develop your approach and techniques, and opportunities for you to embed practice and improvement through increased monitoring, reflection and action planning. All of these mechanisms have been identified by the EEF (2021) as essential contributors to effective professional development.

I end this chapter as I began, encouraging you to focus on *you*: your goals, hopes, habits (be honest!), preferences, beliefs, skills, knowledge and attributes matter. You need to be clear-sighted about these to make active and empowering choices and commitments about the why, how and what of your professional development. Everything you need is within your grasp. Yes, you need to understand and be savvy in navigating the wider context you find yourself in. And, yes, sometimes you'll need to stretch a little (or a lot) to connect to the resources, networks or people that you've identified are necessary for that next step.

However, it starts with you, and guess what?

You've got this! You've already started by reading this chapter and this book.

So, go get a pen and let's continue.

Who and what do you already have?

What next? What first?

If you prefer some more structured questions, to unleash the coach in you, try these:

a   **Goals and intended purpose**: Begin with the end in mind. What is the purpose of your chosen CPD and to what extent does it connect with your goal(s)? How would a supportive or critical friend that knows you well view your intentions?

b   **Determining and measuring impact**: How will you gauge whether your CPD is making a difference and delivering on your intention? When? What indicators might demonstrate progress towards your goal? Is there anyone that you need to share this with? What defines success for you?

c   **Preparing and optimising for success**: What steps can you take to increase your chances of success? What do you need to enhance, leverage or minimise personally and professionally? How can you remain accountable to yourself and others? What does an enabling environment look like for you?

d   **Choosing your 'best bets'**: Given your context and environment, what form of CPD offers the most significant impact given your investment or effort? How can you make the most of your resources? Which research, evidence or guidance might you engage with to choose?

e   **Next Steps**: Assuming success, what could you do next, and why? What might going deeper or further look like? What will you do? How does your CPD journey fit into your long-term career aspirations?

Alternatively, you might prefer these questions adapted from Campbell (2016):

Goals: What do you need to achieve?

Reality: What is happening right now? What is your current context?

Options and opportunities: What could you do? What is available to you?

Will: What will you do? What is your way forward?

Tactics: How will you do it? When will you do it?

Habits: How will you sustain your success? What might get in the way?

References

Adler, N.J. (2016) Want to be an outstanding leader? Keep a journal [online], *Harvard Business Review*. https://hbr.org/2016/01/want-to-be-an-outstanding-leader-keep-a-journal (accessed 30 September 2023).

Boyatzis, R. and Oosten, E.V. (2002) *Developing emotionally intelligent organisations*. www.eiconsortium.org/pdf/developing_emotionally_intelligent_organizations.pdf (accessed 30 September 2023).

Campbell, J. (2016) Framework for practitioners 2: The GROWTH model. In C. van Nieuwerburgh (ed.), *Coaching in professional contexts* (pp. 235–239). London: Sage.

Department for Education (DfE) (2016) *Standard for teachers' professional development*. www.gov.uk/government/publications/standard-for-teachers-professional-development

Easton, L.B. (2008) From professional development to professional learning. *Phi Delta Kappan*, 89(10), 755–759.

Education Endowment Foundation (EEF) (2021) Effective professional development [online]. https://educationendowmentfoundation.org.uk/education-evidence/guidance-reports/effective-professional-development (accessed 25 August 2023).

Guskey, L. (2000) *Evaluating professional development*. Thousand Oaks, CA: Corwin Press.

Miller, P. (2016) White sanction, institutional, group and individual interaction in the promotion and progression of Black and minority ethnic academics and teachers in England. *Power & Education*, 8(3), 205–221.

Miller, P. (2020) 'Tackling' race inequality in school leadership: Positive actions in BAME teacher progression – evidence from three English schools. *Educational Management Administration & Leadership*, 48(6), 986–1006.

Radcliffe, S. (2012) *Leadership plain and simple*, 2nd edition. New York: FT Publishing.

Stoll, L., Handscomb, G. and Harris, A. (2012) *Great professional development which leads to great pedagogy: Nine claims from research*. https://assets.publishing.service.gov.uk/government/uploads/system/uploads/attachment_data/file/335707/Great-professional-development-which-leads-to-great-pedagogy-nine-claims-from-research.pdf (accessed 23 September 2023).

Weston, D., Hindley, B. and Cunningham, M. (2021) *Working Paper: A culture of improvement – Reviewing the research on teacher working conditions*. https://tdtrust.org/wp-content/uploads/2021/02/A-culture-of-improvement_-reviewing-the-research-on-teacher-working-conditions-Working-Paper-v1.1.pdf

Amanda Wilson – Your Career – Your CPD

Amanda Wilson is the headteacher of a one-form entry primary school in south London and has over 20 years' experience in education. She has a passion for supporting teachers and as a qualified coach uses her experience to help individuals become more aware of their abilities and move forward in their careers.

In his 1997 address to the World Bank Conference, the then Secretary-General Kofi Annan said, 'Knowledge is power. Information is liberating. Education is the premise of progress, in every society, in every family' (United Nations, 1997). This quote can be aptly used as a clarion call to Black teachers at all stages in their career; a reminder of the importance of actively seeking out Continuing Professional Development (CPD) opportunities in order to ensure they have the tools needed to progress in their careers.

First and foremost, it's important to note that CPD is not just about going on a course or attending a training session. It's also about shadowing colleagues, leading a department or whole-school project, and even learning about and implementing a new teaching strategy. It's about the professional conversations you have with other teachers, the books you read, the networking opportunities you engage in online or in person. It's about finding ways to increase your knowledge in order to become the best teacher possible; and although that takes a lot of effort, the long-term gain is worth the effort.

As a Black teacher, you need to be willing to put yourself out there and make it known to the powers that be that you want to become the best teacher possible and are willing to work for that accolade. Some Black teachers may not be comfortable with this approach and for good reasons: negative experiences in the past, seeing white teachers being given opportunities that were not offered to the Black teachers, fear of rejection, not knowing exactly how to make your intentions clear, not knowing who to make your intentions known to, not wanting to seem too eager or overly confident in your abilities, or not seeing yourself represented amongst the leadership team and, as such, not believing it's possible. My advice would be to extinguish the negative thoughts and make yourself known to those in senior leadership. Think of it as planting a seed in someone's psyche. You let them know you're interested in developing your knowledge of, say, curriculum development, SEND or school finance, and when an opportunity presents itself, regardless of whether they want to or not, they'll remember the conversation they had with you. It will then be up to you to have a follow-up conversation and establish what the options are for getting involved.

Understandably, the response you receive may not always be a positive one and there are often genuine reasons for that, but if there is one piece of advice I would give, it would be not to allow anyone to tell you that you are not ready, without explaining to you what being ready looks like. The only way you can adequately prepare for the next level is by knowing what you need to do to get there, so ask the question 'what would you suggest I do to get myself ready?', and if they provide constructive feedback, take it on board and run with it. If the feedback is woolly, don't just accept it, ask for clarity.

You should never assume that your school will provide you with CPD opportunities that meet your needs. When I book staff on training, I'm thinking about what that individual needs to support them in their current role and how it will benefit the students they are responsible for during that academic year. I'm not thinking about where that teacher may want to be in five years' time; that's not my priority. But if you want to ensure you give yourself the best start possible, it should be your priority. Consider where you want to get to, what the gaps in your current knowledge are and what you need to do in order to fill those gaps. If you're unsure, ask.

During my third year of teaching, I became interested in coaching and found a Master's-level course that I felt would provide me with the additional skills and knowledge I needed to become more effective at supporting trainee teachers. The course was quite expensive so when I made the pitch to my headteacher, I was clear about how the course would benefit my school, rather than the individual benefits for me.

They say representation matters and never has this been the case more than when it comes to school leadership. As a Black, female headteacher, I am acutely aware that I am one of the 1% of Black headteachers in England and this is even more reason why I would encourage Black teachers to gain as much additional knowledge as possible in order to ensure you're able to make a difference in the school system.

In his 2020 paper, '"Tackling" race inequality in school leadership: Positive actions in BAME teacher progression – evidence from three English schools', Professor Paul Miller (2020) stated:

> As noted by SecEd (2015), '[h]aving a leadership team from a range of ethnic backgrounds also helps to forge good relationships between students and staff'. Students of BAME heritage benefit from seeing staff of BAME heritage in their classrooms and in leadership roles since they provide role models for them.

As Black teachers, when we engage in quality CPD, it's not solely about where it will take us, it's also about the impact it will have on the Black students we engage with both now and in the future. I appreciate that there will be times when it feels like you're banging your head against a brick wall; when the doors to your CPD seem to be locked tight, but it's at times like these that you need to take matters into your own hands and not rely on the school you work in to provide or manage your professional development opportunities.

Compared to 10 years ago, there are so many low-cost CPD opportunities which take place outside of school hours, that teachers have become spoiled for choice. Type the words 'education CPD' into the search bar on Twitter and a whole host of events come up; from TeachMeets to subject-specific conferences – they are all there. There are also a number of organisations whose aim is to provide Black teachers with coaching and support to enable them to adequately prepare for the next stage in their careers: Aspiring Headteachers, which is run by Nadine Bernard, Fig Tree International, which is led by Ann Palmer, BAMEed, Diverse Educators – the list goes on. At times, there may be slightly higher costs involved in some of these training programmes, but the question you should ask yourself is, how much do you value your professional development? Let me give you the answer: your professional development is imperative to the direction you want your career to go in.

It's not about waiting for someone to hand you your CPD plan in a silver-embossed folder and it's also not about waiting for your senior leaders to call you into their offices and tell you about a great course they've seen. If you wait and do nothing, you'll become professionally stagnant. Take the power into your own hands. Decide what it is you want and go after it. If your school supports you, fantastic; if they don't, it's not the end of your journey – in fact, the resilience you show in continuing will be what gets you to where you want to be in the end.

References

Miller, P.W. (2020) 'Tackling' race inequality in school leadership: Positive actions in BAME teacher progression – evidence from three English schools. *Educational Management Administration & Leadership*, 48(6), 986–1006.

SecEd (2015) Improving diversity among leaders. Available at: www.sec-ed.co.uk/best-practice/improving-diversity-among-leaders (accessed 11 March 2019).

United Nations (1997) 'If information and knowledge are central to democracy, they are conditions for development', says Secretary General. UN Press [online], 23 June. https://press.un.org/en/1997/19970623.sgsm6268.html

Big question

What training and development do you need to go for that will help to propel your career in the direction you want it to go in?

9

The Itch

Kemi

I read a newspaper article about the five-year itch and the chances of couples divorcing after five years of marriage increasing. I found this interesting, but I didn't apply the five-year itch to marriage; rather, I applied it to my career as I felt that I wanted to divorce my career as a teacher and move on to something different. I wanted something refreshing, exciting and a new kind of challenge where I could learn, grow and develop in different ways. I was fed up with the same old routine and I was bored of teaching the same curriculum in the same order every year. I always thought people got into a career and they stayed in it until they retired, which is fine if that's what works, but that's not what I wanted for myself. If I were to stay in teaching long term, there had to be progression.

I enjoyed working with young people, but I didn't enjoy teaching any more and I knew that my students deserved someone who was excited about teaching photosynthesis, velocity and titration and that wasn't me. The 'itch' had me in a rut for what seemed like a whole academic year and I felt like I was stagnant. I didn't want to be around let alone involved in the politics of the workplace as well as education. I didn't want to always be on the defensive as a Black woman, or the only Black person in a room, or the only one fighting for Black children. It was tiring. Of course, I wasn't and I'm not naive to the fact that Black people are fighting battles in other sectors, but that was part of my reason for wanting to leave teaching. The 'itch' was a growing snowball of many reasons and remembering my 'why?' wasn't always enough.

There was an article in *The Guardian* which was published in June 2023 which stated that a record number of teachers, 40,000 in England to be exact, had left the profession in 2021–2022 (Adams, 2023). Teacher retention has been a topic of discussion for years, but this record-breaking number post-COVID was astonishing. I wasn't surprised as I had considered leaving the profession due to workload, stress, lack of work–life balance, not enough time to do everything, and so on. I and many others have felt the same, some before five years and some after, but a lot of it boils down to people prioritising themselves and putting their mental health first, which is always the best thing to do.

In my fifth year of teaching, although I felt stuck for the majority of the year, I began evaluating what was working, not working and how to improve or find a solution that would allow me to still work with young people. That's when I started channelling my energy into YBTN and supporting other Black teachers on their career journey, because I knew I couldn't be the only one who felt the way I was feeling. I didn't know what else I could do as a career, so I started YBTN to support others and in turn that helped me on my journey as well. It was a very interesting year for me as a teacher and it opened up my eyes to more that was going on in the world of education and what else I could bring to the table. I was itching for more and knew that I could do more and I'm glad I did, not just for myself, but for others too.

Reference

Adams, R. (2023) Record numbers of teachers in England quitting profession, figures show. *The Guardian* [online], 8 June. www.theguardian.com/education/2023/jun/08/teachers-england-schools-figures-department-education-survey

Caren – When your face no longer fits

What would make a Black teacher choose to abandon their passion and calling? The same reason(s) we need Black teachers in the profession.

Sadly, Black teachers in the UK are leaving the profession at higher rates than their white colleagues due to a complex interplay of factors. Experiences of racial discrimination and microaggressions, documented in studies like the Runnymede Trust's 2020 report, play a significant role. These experiences might manifest as biased performance reviews, limited career advancement opportunities, and the feeling of being unsupported by colleagues or the senior leadership team.

Furthermore, the lack of representation of Black teachers in leadership roles, highlighted in the NASUWT's 2019 report, can lead to feelings of isolation and a lack of belonging. This lack of representation can extend to the curriculum, where the marginalisation of real Black history and perspectives (beyond slavery), create an exhausting environment. This concern is echoed in Henry's 2020 report on the reproduction of inequality. These experiences can further exacerbate feelings of isolation and a lack of 'belonging' for Black teachers, who also feel their students' experiences are not adequately reflected.

In addition to these challenges, Black teachers often find themselves burdened with additional responsibilities related to diversity and inclusion initiatives (anyone up for another BHM 'leadership' role?); mentoring Black students and dealing with racial incidents. This extra racially motivated workload can lead to burnout and dissatisfaction. The combination of these factors can create a hostile and unwelcoming environment, ultimately pushing Black teachers to seek alternative careers where they feel more valued, their contributions are recognised, and their experiences are understood.

I have faced a multitude of these scenarios and have often had to 'grin and bear it', wondering if the skills I acquired in more than 20+ years of education and experience would be utilised adequately.

At times, I have chosen to prioritise my mental health and wellbeing, leaving a role or school where I simply couldn't take it any more. However, as my confidence and time in 'the game' have increased, the sense of mission and responsibility have also increased. I hope that I can be a support to those facing the itch (or ick!) and counsel them to advocate and care for themselves in the midst of a battle, so that they can win the war.

References

Henry, W. A. (2020). 'Schooling, Education and the Reproduction of Inequality: Understanding Black and Minority Ethnic attitudes to learning in two London schools'. Available online: https://repository.uwl.ac.uk/id/eprint/7201/1/W_A_ Henry_2020_REE_-_Schooling%2C_education_and_the_reproduction_of_ inequality_Understanding_black_and_minority_ethnic_attitudes_to_learning_in_ two_London_schools.pdf (last accessed 18 September 2024).

NASUWT (2019). 'Teachers' Mental Health in the UK'. Report available online: https://www.nasuwt.org.uk/static/uploaded/30c31a30-b070-44f1- 8e9f009b650bb350.pdf#:~:text=The%20Big%20Question%202019%20 highlights,and%20mental%20and%20physical%20wellbeing.&text=What%20 are%20the%20concerns%20of%20teachers%3F (last accessed 18 September 2024).

Runnymede Trust (2020). 'Race and Racism in English Secondary Schools'. Report available online: https://cdn.prod.website-files.com/61488f992b58e687f1108c7c/ 61bcc0cc2a023368396c03d4_Runnymede%20Secondary%20Schools%20report%20 FINAL.pdf (last accessed 18 September 2024).

Toby Williams – When the mission no longer aligns

Toby Williams started off as a primary teacher and then sought a new challenge teaching secondary maths in North Manchester. He then became the youngest Assistant Headteacher in the country at the time, running KS4 for an SEMH provision in North London aged just 26. Following his departure from mainstream education, he was then a Learning Program Lead at an edtech unicorn and then within the creative industries.

Teaching was often considered a lifelong career. The spritely, young Newly Qualified Teacher (NQT) is inevitably destined to become the wise veteran. However, that conversation has drastically changed for many reasons and swathes of educators (like myself) are leaving. Research shows that Black teachers, specifically of mathematics, are seen as role models by pupils of all races (Cherng and Halpin, 2016), improve the academic success of students of colour (Dee, 2004; Goldhaber et al., 2019), bridge the gap between communities and maths (Clark et al., 2013; Frank and Hickson, 2018), adapt the curriculum through a more culturally sensitive lens (Frank et al., 2018) and are more likely to persevere in 'difficult' inner-city schools where the pupil population is predominantly Black (Villegas and Irvine, 2010). The value of Black teachers is indisputable. The apparent mass exodus is, too.

The United Kingdom's dire teacher retention crisis is complex, with politics, socio-economics, racism and classism all contributing factors for teachers leaving, irrespective of race. Each individual within the system is affected by this amalgam of factors and, personally, my passion for teaching pupils was inextricably linked to my determination to help and educate those from similar backgrounds to myself.

Personally, I felt that my discontent was two-fold: I did not feel like I fit within the profession and the job had become a never-ending to-do list that took me away from the reason I began teaching, with very little payback.

The constant barrage of planning, marking, observations, meetings and admin for me was demoralising. But I would feel somewhat compensated after having wholesome interactions with, for example, that previously disenfranchised pupil now converted to engaged mathematician (and comedian). As my job as a teacher and then assistant headteacher strayed further from the dissemination of knowledge or building meaningful relationships, I felt dispassionate and indifferent. The bureaucracy and white-centric professionalism I clearly did not fit with. The box-ticking nature of the countless menial tasks that had become teaching

I despised. The skills that I valued myself for were not large stakeholders in my day-to-day role, replaced by dispiriting, monotonous admin. Monotonous admin that, as an adult with ADHD, I could not engage with without continuous never-ending internal frustration and battle.

As I went on, my energy to 'play the game' diminished and my youthful optimism from my PGCE and NQT years had been knocked, and being surrounded by individuals that did not appear to have the actual pupils and their contexts at the heart of what they were doing was not rebuilding my faith in education.

When considering leaving teaching, you fundamentally measure the reasons you wanted the career against the actuality of the career. Research by Richardson and Watt (2005) shows that five main factors are considered when joining teaching: social status, career fit, prior considerations, financial reward and time for family. When the workload, stress and purpose compromise these reasons for joining, it is natural to seek a better-fitting career. I had reached this point and I no longer saw teaching as fulfilling my need for purpose or as a place that was conducive to positive mental health.

I was not the only one from my cohort of once-eager, fresh-faced trainee teachers to be in such a predicament. I studied for my PGCE at a leafy London university as a member of a smaller cohort of student teachers. Of my close friends within this group, half had left the profession after two years and a further quarter (including myself) have left since. We would casually discuss our reasons for abandoning the profession we trained for; we all seemed to cite burnout, being overwhelmed by the workload and unreasonable working hours as reasons. Those that remained had the same experiences but were remaining steadfast, clinging to their original reasons for teaching.

Leaving teaching is not an easy process. I was conflicted because I spent so long conflating leaving the pupils with leaving the teaching profession, and I was not giving my own mental health and happiness the credence they deserved. Instead of taking action, I continued to suffer in silence, becoming increasingly unhappy. At this point, inaction was definitely the wrong choice. Protecting our wellbeing should be a priority, and taking proactive steps to address such a situation is a healthy response. Taking action could have looked like making adjustments in order to realign my work–life balance or seeking a change in employment to completely change my situation.

Fortunately, despite my passivity, based on my career history and experience I was approached and offered a role within the apprenticeship space that utilised my broad array of skills and supported my alternative way of working. I could not leave without knowing that I would still be working towards the personal mission that I had embarked on with teaching, and pursuing a career within the broader education space has met this need whilst valuing myself as a talented professional and respecting my work–life balance. Leaving teaching may not be the solution to all frustrations with the career, however ensuring that you stick to your values and protect your wellbeing in the job that you decide to remain in is key.

References

Cherng, H.Y.S. and Halpin, P.F. (2016) The importance of minority teachers: Student perceptions of minority versus white teachers. *Educational Researcher*, 45(7), 407–420.

Clark, L.M., Badertscher, E.M. and Napp, C. (2013) African American mathematics teachers as agents in their African American students' mathematics identity formation. *Teachers College Record*, 115(2), 1–36.

Dee, T.S. (2004) Teachers, race, and student achievement in a randomized experiment. *Review of Economics and Statistics*, 86(1), 195–210.

Frank, T.J. and Hickson, T.C. (2018) Supporting African-American students in developing positive mathematics identities and achieving success in AP Calculus. *Access and Equity: Promoting High Quality Mathematics in Grades*, pp. 9–12.

Frank, T.J., Khalil, D., Scates, B. and Odoms, S. (2018) Listening to and learning with Black teachers of mathematics. *Rehumanizing Mathematics for Black, Indigenous, and Latinx students*, pp. 147–158.

Goldhaber, D., Theobald, R. and Tien, C. (2019) Why we need a diverse teacher workforce. *Phi Delta Kappan*, 100(5), 25–30.

Richardson, P.W. and Watt, H.M. (2005) 'I've decided to become a teacher': Influences on career change. *Teaching and Teacher Education*, 21(5), 475–489.

Villegas, A.M. and Irvine, J.J. (2010) Diversifying the teaching force: An examination of major arguments. *The Urban Review*, 42(3), 175–192.

Big questions

- What are the reasons for you joining the teaching profession?
- Do you feel fulfilled with the role that you are currently in?
- What would a workplace need to have in regard to values and culture to make you feel valued?

10

Running Away or Moving On

Caren

When one of my best friends told me she was leaving the UK for Dubai, I felt both excited for her and scared that it was only a matter of time before we lost another one of 'us' from the teaching profession. This teacher was fun, feisty and a very gifted educator. Thankfully, she has remained in teaching and even gone on to author a thesis on Black women in education.

There are times when I too have contemplated jumping on a plane and moving to America or Kenya, where I feel I would face fewer challenges; but the students we teach and the perennial reward of helping them achieve – despite their own challenging circumstances – keeps me grounded. One day, I hope I have the courage to board that plane and start a new adventure, taking all I have learned and gained to new horizons.

For many Black teachers venturing abroad, they can often encounter a unique set of experiences and challenges. While they may find opportunities to share their cultural perspectives and enrich diverse classrooms, they can also face biases and stereotypes related to their race. Some may encounter curiosity or ignorance stemming from limited prior exposure to Black individuals, particularly in regions with less racial diversity. However, many Black educators find that teaching abroad allows them to connect with students from different backgrounds, foster cross-cultural understanding, and contribute to global education initiatives. Navigating these cultural differences and adapting to new educational systems can be demanding, but the rewards of personal and professional growth often outweigh the difficulties. Building relationships with colleagues and immersing themselves in the local community can help Black teachers overcome challenges and create fulfilling experiences abroad.

For Black teachers considering teaching abroad, thorough research on the cultural context and educational system of their chosen destination is crucial. Connecting with other Black educators who have taught abroad can provide valuable insights and support. Being open to new experiences, embracing cultural exchange, and maintaining a strong sense of self, can empower Black teachers to thrive in even the most alien of international settings.

Reference

Gourgue, K. (2024) 4 ESL Teaching TIps for Black Teachers, GoAbroad.com [Online]: https://www.goabroad.com/articles/teach-abroad/4-esl-teaching-tips-for-black-teachers (Accessed August 2024).

Kemi

Working in Dubai was one of the best decisions I made for my career as a teacher and SENCO due to the connections I made, preparing to become a member of SLT and most importantly having a work–life balance. I've wanted to work in Dubai since 2016 and I started applying for jobs early that year but with no success. Especially after the five-year itch, working abroad became more of a priority for me. I remember going on one interview for a school in Abu Dhabi and I thought I was close to getting the role, but I was told I didn't have enough experience in behaviour management. I took that on board and worked in a Pupil Referral Unit; it doesn't get more challenging than that if we're talking about behaviour and supporting students with additional needs that were not met in their mainstream settings. However, I still had approximately 300 rejections between 2016 and 2020. Every rejection made me even more determined. I made up my mind in January 2021 that I was going to work in Dubai and absolutely nothing was going to stop me. I reached out to more people who worked in international schools and I asked two headteachers that I had worked with to rip my CV and cover letter apart so I could improve them and use that as a starting point when applying for roles. Of course, I had a good relationship with those headteachers and they were in support of me progressing as they saw I had potential when I had worked with them.

By April 2021, I had three offers and the ball was in my court. I had the opportunity to choose where I wanted to go. I felt like I went from being overlooked to overbooked and I was so grateful to God for the opportunities I had in front of me. I made my decision based on further research of the school, connecting with people who were already working there via LinkedIn and comparing the packages the school had offered me. The school I chose was where I met some amazing people who were so supportive, even beyond the classroom, with adjusting to life in the UAE and settling in. My inclusion team was amazing; my line manager took me under her wing and would advise me on how to think and deal with situations with my 'assistant headteacher cap' on – I wasn't an assistant headteacher yet, but her guidance helped to prepare me for the next stage of my career.

Working in Dubai was where I personally experienced what it meant to have a work–life balance. As always, teachers worked hard, but we were also able to do things for our wellbeing and relax. I found it weird and amazing at the same time that I could go to the beach after school and read a book, or I could meet up with other women I met in Dubai and have a fun ladies' night out. I felt at peace and more relaxed than I had ever felt before in relation to work. We worked as a team and supported one another so things got done on time. Of course, there were times I worked late, but this was not frequent at all.

Moving from the five-day work week to a four-and-a-half-day work week made life even better for me as I could switch off from work after doing what I needed to do and still have my time to myself. It opened my eyes to endless possibilities as I wasn't only meeting and mingling with people who worked in education, but people from various industries, in various roles and walks of life, that I wouldn't have come into contact with if I hadn't moved to Dubai. Maybe part of me was running away from the UK to have a better work–life balance or maybe it was just time for me to move on and experience teaching in a different way and in a different country. Either way, I learned and grew so much as a SENCO. The lessons learned and connections made were invaluable.

Natalie Cole – Navigating highs and lows: A Black teacher's journey in the Middle East and Europe

Natalie Cole is the Head of English at a British International School. She has a decade of teaching experience across London, Bahrain and the Netherlands. Natalie is the founder of The Happy Teacher Hub, an online community and small business dedicated to supporting teachers' wellbeing.

Black teachers leave the profession in greater numbers than their white counterparts. Lack of career progression and diversity of the staff, constant microaggression and intersectional factors (particularly class and race) can be draining for Black teachers and are some of the main reasons they choose to quit teaching (Bradbury et al., 2023):

I chose to leave teaching in London because I felt like the marrow was being sucked out of my bones. I was exhausted from inhabiting a role as more than just a teacher: I was a sister, a parent, a social worker, a solicitor, etc. It was too much and impacted me mentally, socially and, most importantly, the availability I had for my children and myself. I left in order to decide if I still wanted to be a teacher and rediscover who I was. (Black headteacher in Dubai)

Before making the decision to leave teaching completely, some Black teachers are choosing to move internationally as one last shot at continuing in the profession. This number is steadily increasing. In an analysis of Google search data, the international job specialists *Anywork Anywhere* saw an increase of 30% in British expatriates searching for overseas teaching positions in 2021 and 2022 (FE News, 2022). The most searched destination was Dubai, which has repeatedly ranked in the top 10 best places to live and work for expatriates. This is where many teachers, particularly Black teachers, accept teaching positions. Low-income tax, opportunities to travel, accommodation and healthcare paid for by the school, are some of the benefits that attract people to this part of the world. In addition, the increasing diversity makes it an ideal relocation for Black teachers, who have to factor a country's attitudes to race in their decision on where to move.

I started my international journey in Bahrain and had a great experience overall. In 2020, expatriates made up 52.6% of Bahrain's population (News of Bahrain, 2022). While this is mostly made up of Indian and Filipino workers, you will find various other ethnicities within the country. Personally, I never experienced any racial discrimination and felt at ease as a Black British expatriate within the country. However, I believe class contributed more heavily to discrimination than race. Surprisingly, my 'Britishness' and profession seemed to offer me certain privileges and respect that weren't offered to some Indian and Filipino workers in the country.

Fortunately, I was able to progress to middle leadership fairly quickly and was trusted to do the job I was paid to do. However, there are still many barriers for Black teachers in securing leadership roles internationally. In comparison to teaching in the United Kingdom, there are few Black teachers in middle-leadership positions and even fewer in senior leadership:

I decided to move abroad as the UK education system is mentally and physically draining for Black women trying to progress within the system. Constant battles to prove my worth became tiring and demoralising. I chose the Middle East as I had friends and family there, who said positive things about the culture, lifestyle and schools. I wanted to move a few years ago but family commitments meant that I postponed the move. Now I'm in Abu Dhabi, it is still quite apparent that Black teachers are still missing in senior management positions. In my current school, I am one of two Black members of middle management and there are none on the senior leadership team. I'm still happy I moved. I will go home eventually but with the cost of living rising so drastically in the UK and Europe, it felt like the right place to go at the right time. (Black head of psychology, Abu Dhabi)

Although I enjoyed my time in Bahrain, the pull of family and friends made me decide to move to Europe to be closer to them. Fortunately, I was able to find a position at a school in the Netherlands. Before moving to the Middle East, the Netherlands was a place of interest for me. The Dutch are known for maintaining a good work–life balance and the country was rated fifth in the 2022 World Happiness Report. Unfortunately, European schools rarely offer housing or healthcare benefits and there are much higher taxes compared to the Middle East. However, one benefit in the Netherlands is the 30% tax break offered to highly skilled workers for the first five years.

Cities such as Amsterdam, The Hague and Rotterdam have large diverse communities, particularly people from Morocco, Suriname and Turkey (CityDesk, 2023). Although the Netherlands is, for the most part, seen as a liberal and tolerant country, I have personally witnessed prejudice towards Black people and those from the Islamic faith. Unfortunately, I also experienced verbal racism, which left me shaken and angry. An analysis was conducted by Knowledge Platform Integration and Society who reported institutional racism in the housing and labour market, as well as in education and the police force. Those from non-Dutch backgrounds have access to fewer opportunities and face ethnic profiling (European Commission, 2021).

While international schools have students from all over the world, many lack staff that look like the students they teach. I found this more noticeable than I did in Bahrain. When I started, I was one of the only Black full-time members of teaching staff in an organisation of over 200 teachers. At times, this became quite difficult and felt heightened for me after the George Floyd incident. I was overcome with negative emotions with no one to connect with or truly understand what I was feeling at the time. It was both overwhelming and isolating.

Fortunately, progress is being made and there is more work being done in relation to anti-racism training, curriculum and recruitment. Like most other British and British international schools, there is still a long way to go, especially when it comes to career progression for Black teachers. Cultural elitism pervades international schools in the same way it does in Britain, and negatively impacts Black teachers' progression into middle and senior leadership.

Although there are still many barriers faced on the international scene, it still remains one of the best decisions I made for my wellbeing and career. The more Black teachers who decide to take the leap means the international Black community will grow, hopefully allowing more opportunities for us to support, progress and grow together.

References

Bradbury, A., Tereshchenko, A. and Mills, M. (2023) Minoritised teachers' experiences of multiple, intersectional racisms in the school system in England: 'Carrying the weight of racism'. *Race Ethnicity and Education*, 26(3), 335–351.

CityDesk (2023) *Amsterdam is One of the Most Multicultural Cities in the World.* [online] Amsterdam Tourist Information. www.dutchamsterdam.nl/889-more-citizens-and-more-nationalities-in-amsterdam (accessed 31 January 2024).

European Commission (2021) *Institutional racism in The Netherlands* [online]. https://ec.europa.eu/migrant-integration/library-document/institutional-racism-netherlands_en

FE News (2022) Teaching is the most in-demand profession for British expats. FE News [online], 8 July. www.fenews.co.uk/employability/teaching-is-the-most-in-demand-profession-for-british-expats (accessed 31 January 2024).

News of Bahrain (2022) *Sixty-one percent of expat population happy with life in Bahrain* [online]. www.newsofbahrain.com/bahrain/82513.html (accessed 31 January 2024).

World Happiness Report (2022) Happiness, benevolence, and trust during COVID-19 and beyond [online], *World Happiness Report.* https://worldhappiness.report/ed/2022/happiness-benevolence-and-trust-during-covid-19-and-beyond

Grace Anane-Agyei – Embracing change and finding fulfilment in Dubai's classrooms

Grace Anane-Agyei is a co-founder of the education company Xoleio. As well as serving as an examiner for AQA, she has extensive teaching and mentoring experience spanning multiple countries and institutes, providing support in maths and science subjects, financial literacy, exam preparation and scientific projects/dissertation writing for students of all ages.

Having lived and progressed through the British education system, first as a student then teacher, I felt as if I'd become accustomed to a certain way of living and learning. Waking up in the dark, taking the clammy public transport for at least

20 minutes to school, teaching over 100 students whilst shivering in my lab, leaving school early to still end up walking home in the dark to, finally, end up sitting on my sofa in the living room, falling asleep in front of the TV at approximately 5.30pm, or working and/or worrying until late in the evening about all the things that needed to be completed before the next day.

I don't know if it was the lack of sunlight or the cold London-style demeanour from fellow natives but halfway through my NQT year, I'd had enough and wanted more. My fellow NQT colleague, Sarah, admitted to me that she'd felt the same too. I'd met her that year and we'd become instant friends. We were constantly planning lessons together, learning new techniques to teach and assess learning as well as supporting each other with behaviour management. As the stress levels of the role were rising, so was our curiosity and uncertainty about our fit for the profession.

We began speaking to other teachers and heads of departments all over the borough to understand exactly where our concerns about teaching had risen from: Were we feeling inadequate as teachers or were we not being supported enough? Was it to do with the behaviour of our students within our borough, class or school? The techniques that we were taught to use: were they outdated or simply too innovative? Were the constant, overwhelming marking expectations taking over our lives? Or was our love for teaching just simply not strong enough to look past all the frustrating aspects of the job that were keeping us from focusing on the progress of the kids?

We knew that within us lay an innate care for our students: we wanted every young person we encountered to feel safe, supported, encouraged and acknowledged. Despite the stress that came with teaching, we didn't want to simply walk away. We were fully aware of the profound impact we aimed to create for the future generation.

Our search for solutions had brought us to a few other teachers who had been fantasising about and glamourised the lives of expat teachers to the point where I believed they were in a completely different line of work to us. I was convinced that, before hanging up my board pens and lab coat after such a short time, I would need to give teaching abroad a try. I wasn't too fussy with where I would move to, but I knew it would need to be somewhere warm that was not void of sunlight for 70% of the year. It was Sarah who first suggested the UAE. She asked if I would be willing to accompany her and I started packing my bags in response. When I had started telling a few people that moving to Dubai was a definite option for me, what I received was an excessive amount of backlash, concern, fear and discouragement. A huge amount of the negative statements made were directly linked to my skin and/or gender. I had family members stating concern for my safety 'as a woman' and claiming that I wasn't aware of the 'kind of country' I was moving to; I had friends questioning my sanity, telling me that the 'racism in the UK is already excessive; why would I want to move to the Middle East?' Even upon informing my head of department about my decision to move, he had said to me 'teaching is going to be so different out there for you as a female teacher, I think it would be better if you stayed'. At the time, I had worried that these people, most of whom had never been to the UAE, could possibly be right. Absolutely ridiculous. Moving to Dubai is one of the greatest blessings God has granted me.

I have worked in different private schools in the heart of the city. Presently, as of 2023, I have been teaching here for five years, have gained experience as deputy head of my department, head of house, have signed up to tutor for three different tuition companies, all of which allow me to make triple the usual tuition rate in the UK and I have co-founded an education company of my own.

From a day-to-day teaching aspect, not much of the role is different. I am still inundated with marking, meetings, data deadlines, and emails. I still adhere to the British curriculum and teach content from a British exam specification. I follow British safeguarding policies within my school, ensuring the safety of all my students, and I am still expected to plan/teach outstanding lessons. If I wanted to work in an American school or Emirati public school in the same city, I could easily encounter different expectations and teaching styles. Teaching abroad, just to this one country so far, has opened my eyes to the possibilities and opportunities that the profession can offer me; I've considered moving further east to China or Thailand. I've had unique educational experiences that have helped me to consider how I might develop my own school in Ghana, especially since I've found progression easier and more attainable in the UAE. I've been able to learn from the country's culture, the history and even taken time to learn the Arabic language.

The key difference for me, that has affirmed my continued stay in the UAE, is the difference in pay and standard of living. For teachers, there is a lot of work that must be done to support our students, and it never seems to end, so finding a suitable work–life balance can be difficult. Personally, in the UK, it felt near impossible. However, in Dubai, with the great weather, the countless activities and events available, the huge mix of people from all walks of life and different nationalities, I find I never fall short of things to do and, at times, must actively block out weekends in my diary for isolation and rest. I've also found time to travel, seeing more of Asia (cheap flights from here to Thailand!), I have a beautiful apartment, a lovely community of friends who have quickly become family, a cute young kitten (everyone who sees her describes her as cute so it must be true), and I'm ambitiously aiming to save money to buy my own villa, which feels truly attainable as, in comparison to the wage I'd be earning in the UK at my current level of experience, I am taking home eight times more money every month. The future feels brighter.

There are many different challenges that come with the job, so to say teaching in one country is completely stress-free and better than another wouldn't be fair; at least not when comparing a handful of schools in Dubai to a handful of schools in London. Instead, I find that it's best for the individual teacher to figure out what they may no longer appreciate or can no longer tolerate from within the profession and work their way towards finding the role that can accommodate their needs and cultivate their strengths whilst supporting them and providing an environment they can genuinely thrive in. In other words, this is your sign to move abroad before everywhere else gets more expensive!

Petal Darnley – She who cries loudest

Petal Darnley teaches Business and Economics at a British International School in Dubai. She started her career as an LSA, before completing her PGCE. She then went on to secure her first teaching role at a school in South London before moving to Dubai in 2017. Her experience in education has been a rollercoaster to say the least and, like so many, she has thought of an exit plan but is also passionate about supporting young people.

Now, let me start out by saying I love working in the classroom. Working with young people has not only been my bread and butter, but it has also ignited enthusiasm and passion I didn't know I had in me to give to a job. But that's the thing about being a teacher, it's not just a job. It becomes the way you think, the way you feel, the way you communicate and solve conflict in every aspect of life.

Before I delve further into my adventures in the classroom, let me tell you a little bit more about myself. I was born in Guyana and lived there until I was 10 years old. I moved to London to join my mum and dad who had settled there three years prior. I loved school, not so much the learning part but the social circles I built lifelong connections with.

My first classroom teacher position was at a well-known 'good' school in south London, that I thoroughly enjoyed. It was the most diverse institution I had ever stepped foot in; teachers hailed from all religions, ethnicities, cultures and sexualities. So, when I announced to my family and friends that I would be moving to Dubai for a new teaching job, they were shocked to say the least. I left teaching in the UK in search of opportunities to soak up more of what the world had to offer, and securing the position in Dubai meant that I could do that and the job I loved and make more money for my family too.

The first thing I noticed on my first day at work at my brand-new, shiny private school in the UAE is that I was the only Black teacher in the staff meeting. There was no one else there in secondary that was the same as me. Now, I must be explicit and say secondary because there was one other. I later found out that there was one other Black female teacher in primary. For added context, most private international schools in Dubai are through schools so children aged 5–18 and staff often share the same campus and facilities. So, out of all 274 primary and secondary staff there were two Black people; this surprised me as there were Black people in Dubai and Black students at the school. I felt out of place and alone for the first time in a school environment and I didn't just feel that way, I was treated that way too – often left out of team socials and office banter so, ultimately, I left that school for another one in Dubai. I was not ready to give up on my dream yet.

My journey into middle leadership seemed to happen by chance, a case of 'right place, right time', or the only person with a particular subject experience so the default option. I started out as Second in Charge of Faculty, at a school that was a tad more diverse than the first. This time there were two Black secondary teachers and a few more teachers who were not just the standard white British; the staff were a lot friendlier and more inclusive, so I felt a little more at ease at work.

Although I knew I was the default choice for the job, nonetheless it was my time to shine. I know this course through and through and had experience turning around student progress and outcomes. But this was a step into management, something I was not prepared for, therefore harder than expected. It was not just the workload but changing staff's mindset towards the way they approached the course. Staff struggled to meet deadlines and failed in almost every quality assurance check. I raised this with my line manager over and over again. Begging for support and middle-leader training, I needed help with getting the team to take a more proactive approach to delivering the course. So, I did the work myself, mostly completing staff's assessment paperwork and chasing students for missing tasks. When I shared the hours I had put into this, I sometimes got a thank you. I felt like I could not complain anymore. After all, I was often reminded that this was my remit, my responsibility, and I would be held accountable if we failed verification. Nothing ever changed so I sucked it up and got on with it, spending long hours after work and on weekends correcting mistakes.

Why didn't I seek help or complain about my challenges further? I could have spoken to my line manager's line manager, but this is not an option you feel is available to you as a Black woman in the workplace. There is always a profound fear of appearing lazy or voicing your frustrations in a way that can be deemed aggressive.

Two years later, I was promoted to head of faculty and quickly looked to my team to appoint a new second. Only one stepped forward, an eager young teacher who was the right person for the job anyway. She is organised, enthusiastic and willing to get stuck in. She is Irish, comes from a family of educators, so I thought it was only natural that she would look to climb the ladder. She took up the management of the course I was previously charged with. Remembering how challenging it was for me, I blocked out an hour a week where she could pop in and get the guidance and support needed to effectively manage the course. I wanted to be the person I wish I had as second in charge.

Head of faculty was really my chance to develop into the middle leader I always wanted to be and, at first, I really looked forward to my weekly line manager meeting. This was my opportunity to meet with a senior leader, who has been in my position before and would be an excellent mentor and role model to guide me to success. The first thing I noticed was how focused these meetings were on the second in charge. I was constantly asked, is she getting enough support? Is she getting enough opportunity to prepare her for becoming head of faculty one day? What do I do to make sure she does not feel like the course is solely her responsibility? The opposite of what I felt I experienced as second.

As we got further into the academic year and deadlines were approaching, my second in charge was feeling the pressure. It is hard getting other members of staff in line to get the job done. She complained, as she should do. My line manager asked for an urgent meeting after school. She wanted me to prove that I had been helping my second. What evidence do I have? 'Meeting minutes'. She should never feel like she is the only one is charge: 'She is not the only one in charge'. She should not be staying after school, working on weekends and constantly chasing other staff members on her own: 'She's not'.

Why were her cries for help worth an urgent meeting and demand for support, but mine weren't?

Helen Debrah-Ampofo – Why I left the UK for the UAE

Helen is an English teacher from London who left the UK for the UAE in 2017. She is a wife, mother and entrepreneur who helps expat women with their natural hair find the right products and services they need. She can always be found with a good book and enjoying good food.

At age 18, I moved from London to Nottingham for university. It was different from what I was used to but I embraced the change and eventually fell in love with life outside of London. Nottingham, like many other places in England that I had now branched out to, was slower-paced and less busy than my hometown. And, most importantly, my money stretched a lot further.

Growing up in London, it used to be £4 for a weekly bus pass. Then they introduced the Oyster card and it was free for everyone who was still in some form of education until the age of 18. After university, I was shocked at the amount I had to pay now that I was an adult. Some of my friends would have to take Transport for London (TfL) loans from work in order to afford the ever-rising costs of transport in London. But they didn't even bat an eyelid. This was normal in London. However, in Nottingham, even my rent cost less than this. I knew it didn't have to be this way as life outside of the capital was much more reasonably priced (I paid £162.50 a month for rent!).

My boyfriend-at-the-time and I both became teachers around 2012–2013. In Nottingham, the starting salary for teachers was around £21,000, whereas it was approximately £27,000 in London. Although we were both born and raised in London, guess where we chose to begin our teaching careers? The London weighting would have been lost on transport, rent and 'keeping up with the Jones'.

For me, a good quality of life is the priority.

Teaching in Nottingham was not without its issues though. I worked in two inner-city schools in Nottingham and in both schools, even though the pupils were diverse, Black teachers were heavily underrepresented.

There are a number of reasons why this was, and still is, the case. It could be due to institutional racism in that Black people may not continue through the education system long enough to reach university, graduate and then become teachers. We know Black people underachieve in the UK education system and appear to plateau at university, graduating with grades far below their educational potential. It could be due to our parents putting pressure on us to become doctors, lawyers and engineers but never teachers.

I found that when we are represented, we are deemed as good with 'behaviour management' and are pushed towards more pastoral roles within school. When we do come across Black employees at school, many of them are pigeon-holed into 'head of year' roles or are 'key workers' in the behavioural units of schools. How many of us break through to a senior leadership team (SLT) or become a headteacher?

The pastoral responsibilities placed on Black teachers, particularly in inner-city schools, mean we are not only educators of our subjects but also become parents and social workers to the children in our care. Many of us identify with our pupils – we used to be them 10 years ago – and so we work ourselves hard in order to support them and 'make a difference'. Most of us came into teaching for these children. We know firsthand, as an ethnic minority ourselves, that having a Black teacher who 'understood us' would have made a huge difference. And so we go all out until we eventually burn out.

Compounded by large class sizes, the often cold, dark weather and a general lack of respect for the teaching profession, is there any wonder there is an exodus of Black teachers leaving?

We are doing the most and earning the least.

As a 20-something-year-old who was eager to please, I was more than happy to be at work from 7am to 7pm, trying to get everything done on my to-do list. I never did. But now, as a mother in my 30s and with 20-20 hindsight vision, I know there is absolutely no way I should have done this. I don't know of any other profession where there is an expectation to get essential work done outside of working hours. We are working for free. Unfortunately, our African upbringing often means we respect and submit to authority even when we are being overworked and underpaid. We are also far too accustomed to struggle stories as part of our narrative and working 'twice as hard to get half as far'.

But deep down, I knew it didn't have to be this way.

I remember getting flurries of emails from agencies advertising teaching abroad. I had already left London for a better quality of life and these emails made it seem as though if I went even further, paradise was waiting. My boyfriend had become my husband by then and he, too, was being hunted for teaching jobs overseas. We had no dependents at the time and so started to seriously contemplate life abroad. We were both accepted into an agency in London who managed to place my husband in a school in Abu Dhabi. I wasn't able to work as an English teacher in Abu Dhabi unfortunately, because they wanted my degree to be in English rather than psychology but we decided to make the move anyway.

The medical cover, housing allowance, salary and other benefits in the UAE for us worked out to be more than one teacher's salary in the UK (in both Nottingham and London). Plus, the class sizes were smaller, the sun shone all year round and the profession was largely appreciated; it was a no-brainer for someone who prioritises a good quality of life.

The plan was to be abroad for two years. We wanted to make enough money to pursue other passions on our return to the UK. At the time of writing, this is now my seventh year in the region and I am working as an English teacher in an international school in Dubai. I have no plans for repatriation any time soon.

When I trained as a teacher in 2012–13, the rate of teacher retention was five years. I know I wouldn't be a teacher if I were still in the UK – the conditions make it almost impossible to stay for so long. It is also clear, after being in a completely different educational system, that much more can be done to improve the lives of teachers in the UK. We do a tough job and are the backbone of society, which many people witnessed during the pandemic, however we are undervalued, underpaid and underappreciated in the UK.

We know that the wellbeing of our students is not the responsibility of the Black educator alone as much more can be done before our students reach our classroom. We are exploited because we genuinely care about young people. However, we are becoming more aware, from the decision to scrap free school meals during the height of the pandemic – at a time when children needed it the most – that the UK government could do so much more to lighten the load for us all, but refuse to do so. We are working in a broken system and no matter how much we kill ourselves, we cannot do it all.

We went into education to make a difference and we can to a great deal of young people, however it is but a drop in a very large ocean. It may be better to leave and earn enough money to survive; after all, how will we take care of others if we do not take care of ourselves first?

Aaron T. Senessie NPQLT – Am I where I want to be?

Aaron Senessie is a mathematics teacher with over 10 years' teaching experience at state, private, inner London and suburban schools. This also includes teaching internationally in the USA, in North Carolina, before returning to the UK to commence his current role as Head of Mathematics and Computing at an inner London school.

So far, I have never stayed more than three years in a role. My biggest move came four years into my career when I decided to migrate from my comfortable life as a UK maths teacher to become a US math (without the 's') teacher.

What made me leave? I actually loved the role and the school I was in. It offered me opportunities and experiences I never thought I would have. It just so happened that the year before I left I was overlooked for two promotions. I couldn't say whether the reasons were valid or not but I became aware that I had hit a ceiling. So, when the opportunity for a move presented itself it didn't take much convincing. It also allowed me the chance to achieve a significant life goal, so I jumped on it.

Teachers who have moved jobs more than once will understand that moves come with their challenges, especially if the school you're moving to has a high staff turnover. This is why, before I move jobs, I have to really consider a number of things. One of the advantages you have when you're applying for a job in the UK is that you get to walk the halls of your prospective new place of employment. You meet the students, your department and shake the hands of any of the senior leaders you happen to pass in the corridor. This is supposed to give you an idea of what it's like to be there on a day-to-day basis. But you don't really know a school until you turn up day in, day out.

Of the schools that I have previously taught at, I have had to deal with racially charged issues at two of them. Both events were as avoidable as they were unexpected, as up until that point I had not witnessed any overt racism in either school. The events were brought on by white guys wanting to impress their younger (mostly non-Black) class, maybe in a vain attempt to be seen as a rebel. This is not something you would be able to foresee from your interview day.

When I relocated, I moved to a southern US state and anyone with a basic knowledge of the history of the USA knows that The South is where a majority of the 'bad stuff' happens. As I never actually visited the school before I accepted the job, I was very apprehensive about what I was signing myself up to. One thing that did calm my nerves was that there was a Black female on the interview panel – she was the vice principal and her being there relieved a lot of my anxiety. Luckily, in hindsight, when I consider where I was in my career at the time of my move, I would say that I definitely moved on at the right time. I had a clear idea of what I wanted to achieve in my career and it required me to move. Any temptation I may have had to remain in the UK wasn't helped by the conditions that teachers in the UK found themselves working in. It was not long after Michael Gove had been moved out of his role as Secretary of State for Education and you could still feel the effects of his policies. It was also during Michael Wilshaw's tenure as Head of Ofsted. Performance-related pay was introduced, teacher workloads prompted resignations, which in turn led to an even higher teacher workload, there were increasing behaviour management issues, unrealistic results were expected (shout out Fischer Family Trust 5), Ofsted inspections were constantly looming and then there was the prospect of academisation (I later came to believe that this may not be the worst thing in the world).

You will never be in a job where you will agree with everything that goes on, whether that be the teaching philosophy, behaviour management, teacher workload, culture or colleagues. This is then compounded when you consider the microaggressions that come with race.

Working as one of the only Black members of staff, you are always mindful of playing into stereotypes and of preventing yourself from being easily scapegoated. I once attended a conference run for Black teachers and one thing that

stuck with me was the shared pressure to work overtime to buck the precon-
ceived notions of who you are and what you are capable of doing. For example,
I always wore a shirt and tie, even on dress-down Fridays, as a way of ensuring
that there was no space for anyone to ever question my professionalism.

What happens when the pressure in a job becomes too much? What do I do
if I feel inadequate in my job? What if things are consistently not going my way?
All teachers feel this way at some point. I tell all of my PGCE students, trainees
and ECTs that one thing about this profession is that it is very personal. A profession like this is very intimate; it picks at your very being so when things go
wrong, and they often do, you take it extremely personally. How should you
react? Do you get up and run? I hate that term! 'Running away'.

When people are unhappy and do not see things getting better, they tend to
leave. In my experience, it's never one specific incident that pushes a person to
leave; even ongoing conflict with management doesn't necessarily result in a
resignation letter. It is fundamental disagreements, inaction or inconsistencies
that drive people out of jobs.

I would class my departure from one of my previous schools as running away.
I'll set the scene. New headteacher with all that entails – new view, new policies,
new direction and new philosophy. To this day, I have to state, I have never
personally been treated *extremely* badly by any principal or headteacher. But in
this case, I saw the tide out at sea and I was not waiting around for it to hit me.
So, I abandoned ship.

I don't regret leaving when I did. It was during a learning walk that I realised
I had to leave. The headteacher spoke to a student in my class about the regular-
ity of my marking. He said something along the lines of 'he doesn't mark your
work much, does he?' to which the student replied 'yes, he does, he is really
good'. In that moment I realised that even though I was breaking my back to be
an 'outstanding' teacher, it would probably never be enough. In context, I should
also mention that earlier on that year I had been graded a 'three' (requires
improvement) in my lesson observation and put on a teacher support plan; I was
two months into my NQT year. When I now consider the new teachers I support
in my current role, that should never have happened to me. I shudder every time
I remember that graded observations were commonplace; this in itself probably
pushed a significant number of teachers out of the profession. Staying in that
environment would not have been healthy.

In teaching, as in life, you pick your hand. Every job is difficult in one way or
another, which is why I would encourage you to ensure that whenever you go
to an interview the school is as good a fit for you as you are for it. A principal I
worked for once introduced himself as 'a father first and a principal second'. I
now do the same; the job, even though it is extremely important to me, is never

the whole me. As with every job, you work to live, so there are some things you need to prioritise, yourself being one. So, when deciding if you are moving on or running away, consider these Big Questions.

Big questions

- Can I find a school that supports me and my purpose more than this current one?
- At this stage in life, what do I need?
- Do I know myself, and what are the philosophies I really believe in? Are they supported here?
- Am I inspired to be my best?
- Does the school actually need or value my skills?

11

To BAME or not to BAME?

Kemi and Caren – The inadequacy of 'BAME' in education

To BAME or not to BAME? Now, that really is the question.

The term BAME (Black, Asian and Minority Ethnic) has been widely used as a catch-all descriptor for non-white individuals in the UK since the 1980s. However, its use in educational discourse is increasingly criticised for its inherent flaws and potential to cause harm.

Although the acronym aims to be inclusive of ethnic minorities in the UK, it's an umbrella term that homogenises vastly diverse ethnic groups with distinct needs and experiences into essentially two categories: white British and other. That is too simplistic and unfair to different ethnic groups, as it effectively eradicates individual and group experiences. We must also consider how the term BAME distorts the statistics when it comes to the issues affecting Black people and other ethnicities disproportionately. When we read an article about BAME people, we don't always get the full facts and percentages of the ethnicities that are being discussed. Instead, we get an overall summary, or a figure that still needs to be analysed further.

Grouping together individuals of differing cultural, religious and linguistic backgrounds in education further obscures the critical disparities in attainment, or the challenges faced by specific ethnic groups (Laux and Nisar, 2022). For example, teachers using BAME may overlook the success of Chinese students, whilst failing to address the underachievement of Pakistani students.

Furthermore, the term BAME perpetuates an 'othering' effect, positioning ethnic minorities against a white majority norm. This can reinforce feelings of marginalisation, hindering both students' sense of belonging and teachers' cultural understanding of the nuances (National Museums Liverpool, n.d.). Additionally, for families and the wider community schools serve, the term can mask their specific identities. Parents may feel their specific cultural heritage is dismissed, hindering effective school–family partnerships that are critical for student success.

Instead of BAME, educators should strive for more specific and nuanced language that acknowledges the diversity within ethnic groups. This will lead to targeted support interventions, culturally responsive teaching and increased equity in schools, where diversity is recognised and respected.

Our experiences as Black women are different from the experiences of an Asian man and other ethnic groups. It is not universal and we need to be sensitive to the fact that our experiences are not all the same. We cannot speak for all Black people and we definitely cannot speak for every ethnicity that comes under BAME.

Some schools feel that as long as they have a member of staff that is non-white, they have done their part for society, ticked their diversity box and met their diversity quota. However, it's not that simple and we can't reduce our individual, historic and group contributions to a monolithic term like BAME.

Yes, the term BAME was not created to be divisive. However, in this day and age, we need to acknowledge that it is dated and can be problematic as many people don't subscribe to it. Even the government has acknowledged, as of May 2022, that it is no longer using the term BAME as 'terms like "BAME" (Black, Asian and minority ethnic) were no longer helpful' (Laux and Nisar, 2022). It recommended that this term (and other oversimplistic terms) should be dropped; advocating instead for a focus on understanding disparities and outcomes, such as in education or health – 'for specific ethnic groups'.

Hear! Hear!

References

Laux, R. and Nisar, S. (2022) Why we've stopped using the term 'BAME' in government. *Civil Service Blog* [online], 19 May. https://civilservice.blog.gov.uk/2022/05/19/why-weve-stopped-using-the-term-bame-in-government (accessed 7 March 2024).

National Museums Liverpool (n.d.) *Why we're no longer using BAME*. www.liverpoolmuseums.org.uk/stories/why-were-no-longer-using-bame (accessed 7 March 2024).

Aisha Thomas – I am more than a four-letter acronym

Aisha Thomas is a former assistant principal, responsible for diversity, equity and inclusion. Aisha provides training on race in education at the University of Bristol, the University of the West of England and in schools nationwide. In 2018, she presented a documentary for the BBC, investigating the low number of Black teachers in Bristol, and in 2019, Aisha delivered a powerful TEDxBristol talk called 'Why Representation Matters'. Aisha is currently working on a number of local and national projects, including Beyond the 26, which collects stories and experiences from Black and minority educators in Bristol. She has also contributed to a series of videos on allyship for BBC Teach. For more information, follow @itsrepmatters on social media and visit www.repmatters.co.uk

The question of appropriate language use has always been an interesting one. I could wax lyrical about all the possible ways to describe me … Black, BAME, BME, Global Majority, racially minoritised, melanin rich, N-word … The list goes on. Yet, when I think about my white counterparts, the list ends swiftly. To be racialised as white is to be human; it is the starting point, or so we are led to believe. We live with the existence of race as a social construct, yet many still do not understand the implications of this today.

To be described as BAME (Black Asian minority ethnic) is to be othered, is to be told that I do not belong and that I am not valued. It is an immediate othering of my existence; if I am not white British, then I can be lumped into a bucket with everyone else who is non-white British, yet I know that all of our individual lived experiences are not one and the same. Yet we have seen the continued use of the term. The first use of the word occurs in Hansard in 2004 (HC Deb, 2004), with the term overtaking the use of BME. Zamila Bunglawala said 'Please, don't call me BAME or BME!'. Bunglawala explains how, while acronyms 'can be very catchy and convenient', they can be widely misunderstood, have 'negative connotations' and be 'hurtful to people' (Bunglawala, 2019).

The term is problematic for a number of reasons. Often, white ethnic minorities such as Gypsy Roma are not always associated with BAME, due to the racialisation of their skin as white, yet we know that they are among some of the most marginalised and disadvantaged communities. Exclusion of these communities is to marginalise them further. The term also opened the door for a skewing of data; in 2020, when Matt Hancock was asked to name Black cabinet members, he named Rishi Sunak and Priti Patel as BAME (HuffPost UK, 2020). Using a wider 'catch-all phrase' opens the door to the erasure of the drawn data and is therefore an appropriate response to the issue in hand. The Department for Education supported this by stating, 'We do not use the terms BAME (Black, Asian and minority ethnic) and BME (Black and minority ethnic) because they emphasise certain ethnic minority groups (Asian and Black) and exclude others (mixed, other and white ethnic minority groups). The terms can also mask disparities between different ethnic groups and create misleading interpretations of data' (UK Government, 2021). Whilst this may be the perspective of some, there are still organisations such as BAMEEd, Operation Black Vote and the Runnymede Trust, who have said that it can sometimes create unity amongst minority communities.

What is clear is that many feel the term is outdated and no longer helps when considering steps to becoming racially literate, and taking the time to ask an individual how they would like to be racialised is much more appropriate. However, in moments where data collection is needed, some may still reach for the term, because they are yet to find a useful alternative. I personally use the terms racialised and racially minoritised to acknowledge that race is a projected social construct. However, terms like Global Majority are just as useful. Members of the Global Majority are Black, Indigenous, Latinx, Pacific Islander, South Asian, South-east Asian and many more – all of which are not the minority.

References

Bunglawala, Z. (2019) Please, don't call me BAME or BME! Civil Service Blog [online], 19 May. https://civilservice.blog.gov.uk/2019/07/08/please-dont-call-me-bame-or-bme

HC Deb (15 January 2004) vol. 416 col. 854W. https://hansard.parliament.uk/Commons/2004-01-15/debates/7167ea0d-b895-4697-8e4c-812b66a2527e/Ethnicity (accessed 31 January 2024).

HuffPost UK (2020) Matt Hancock names two Asians when asked to identify Black cabinet members [online], 7 June. www.huffingtonpost.co.uk/entry/black-cabinet-matt-hancock-protests_uk_5edc9ffdc5b6aedebbc6a27a (accessed 31 January 2024).

Thomas, A. (2022) *Representation matters: Becoming an anti-racist educator.* London: Bloomsbury.

UK Government (2021) *Style guide: Writing about ethnicity.* www.ethnicity-facts-figures.service.gov.uk/style-guide/writing-about-ethnicity (accessed 31 January 2024).

Interrupting Racism – social media account (Instagram)

Wonu Adedoyin-Salau – The detail in diversity

Wonu is an assistant headteacher at an East London secondary school and sixth form. Passionate about parity of experience and the transformative power of English, she has contributed to significant reform in her school to create a curriculum that is representative, rigorous and invites students to engage in critical discourse.

Black, Asian and Minority Ethnic or BAME is a term that has historically been used to identify people from the Global Majority. The very fact that the term acronymises a group of people from such diverse backgrounds is the main reason I find it problematic. To lump languages, cultures, traditions into a 'digestible' term is not only unhelpful but a way of upholding the notion that whiteness is normative and people from Global Majority backgrounds are some sort of monolithic other, with identical experiences who face identical prejudices. This is just not true.

In March 2021, the Commission published their report into racial and ethnic disparities in the UK (Commission on Race and Ethnic Disparities, 2021). Encouragingly, the Commission recognised the need to do away with the term 'BAME', citing that 'the term "BAME community" feels like a group that is held together by no more than what it is not' (Commission on Race and Ethnic Disparities, 2021). As educators, this becomes even more apparent when you consider the different cultural experiences of our students. While it is important to recognise that a monolithic term homogenises an experience that is vast and varied, it is also imperative to see our students as individuals who may, unfortunately, be more susceptible to certain experiences because of their specific ethnic backgrounds.

My secondary school had students from a diverse range of backgrounds. The Indian and Pakistani girls tended to be from more affluent families whose grandparents could also claim the title of 'Asian British', while many of the Black African girls belonged to families who had immigrated to the UK just before or soon after their births. Under the banner of BAME, it could be presumed that as second- and third-generation children, our school experience would be considered homogenous. However, this 'subtle' difference shaped my entire school experience.

My family, like many other Black Africans in the early 2000s, migrated from the inner-city to the suburbs, more specifically Essex. Our communities were less established and this sometimes made school quite an isolating experience. In our school, like many schools across the country, the Black girls, whether consciously or unconsciously, were treated differently. Our laughter was always treated as boisterous rather than jovial, our inquisitiveness labelled as defiance and impertinence. I became acutely aware of the fact that, not only were we different from the white and Asian girls, we were, by some teachers, considered as threats to decorum and civility in the classroom. Were there explicit policies policing hair styles? No, not necessarily, but I do distinctly remember one of my friends being told that she should have put her hair up in a 'nice bun' after sporting her freshly washed afro to school. An innocent comment? Maybe. A microaggression? Absolutely. The idea that her hair would look better in a 'nice bun' was enough to remind her that her hair's natural state was a deviation from the norm and contributed to the various ways in which she felt othered.

The differences between the treatment of Black students and students from Global Majority communities is something that we must pay attention to. Categorising all of these groups contributes to the erasure of individual experience, especially where ethnic identity is concerned. Another poignant example of why it's important to consider the individual experiences of Black children is the widely publicised case of Child Q.

In the summer of 2020, a young Black female student was strip-searched by female police officers; this included a search of her intimate body parts without an appropriate adult present. Child Q's case shocked the nation. How could such a thing happen to a child? Was this level of violation really necessary? Why did no one prioritise her need to be safeguarded?

The City Hackney Safeguarding Children Partnership (*Local Child Safeguarding Practice Review: Child Q*) concluded that 'Having considered the context of the incident, the views of those engaged in the review and the impact felt by Child Q and her family, racism (whether deliberate or not) was likely to have been an influencing factor in the decision to undertake a strip search' (CHSCP, 2022: 6).

This bleak conclusion is another reminder to many about the premature adultification of Black boys and girls. Not only is it highly probable that this would not have occurred if she was a white girl, but it is likely that it would not have happened if she were an Indian, Filipino, Chinese or Polish girl. The irony here is that, if we persisted in using the term BAME, it would help to perpetuate the erasure of the unique prejudices that each respective group is more susceptible to. It is particularly important for educators to identify how these conscious and unconscious biases may cause us to project our own expectations onto students because of what we believe is 'normative' for students belonging to their cultural/ethnic group.

In 2020, the term 'decolonising the curriculum' became central to many discussions about curriculum design and curriculum intent. Naturally, like many schools, we also wanted to reevaluate our curriculum choices in light of this. As a school that is multicultural and multi-ethnic, we felt that it was important to have a curriculum that not only challenged students but also made them feel that they were a part of a wider global narrative. It would be unfair to say that this work around diversity started in 2020 because it did not. For many English teachers, it started in 2000 when AQA introduced a new cluster of poems called, 'Poetry from Different Cultures' (AQA, 2002). This rich anthology included poems from talented British writers such as Grace Nichols and John Agard. This was an attempt to meet the Labour party demands for education reform and their desire to see an English curriculum that was rich in diversity. This great triumph was soon met with great defeat just 10 years later when then Education Secretary, Michael Gove, published changes to the national curriculum (DfE, 2013), including the exclusion of non-British writers in the KS4 curriculum.

As a recently qualified teacher, I remember how this announcement was greeted with horror and disappointment by my more experienced colleagues. They felt it was purposefully exclusionary and a top-down attempt to stop students from being exposed to a rich history of literature. At the time, I could not quite understand their outrage nor did I have the foresight to recognise the possible implications for our curriculum, but I soon would.

Sadly, some students go through their entire education never seeing themselves in this grand narrative of the 'English canon' because the narrative, while grand, is not always representative of the Global Majority. While labels such as Black, Asian and White can be seen as a hindrance, we still live in a world where racism significantly affects how educational policy is interpreted and applied. It would be remiss of us to assume that our Ghanaian, Jamaican, Bengali and Irish students sit next to each other and use the exact same cultural experiences to engage with the curriculum. This is a fallacy that amplifies the futility of the BAME label. It does not and cannot sufficiently express the multiplicity of thought, the rich history of tradition and the lived experiences in contemporary Britain.

An anti-racist curriculum should engender a culture of inclusion, representation and appreciation for the varied and complex backgrounds of our young people, and that is why we need to do away with this archaic and reductive term. We need curricula that are not simply diversified in an attempt to tick a box or fulfil a quota, but rather that reflect the world and the rich tapestry of experience that surrounds us.

References

AQA (2002) *AQA GCSE English and English literature anthology*. Oxford: Oxford University Press.

CHSCP (2022) *Local child safeguarding practice review: Child Q*. [online] https://chscp.org.uk/wp-content/uploads/2022/03/Child-Q-PUBLISHED-14-March-22.pdf (accessed 10 May 2022).

Commission on Race and Ethnic Disparities (2021) *Summary of recommendations.* [online] Gov.uk. www.gov.uk/government/publications/the-report-of-the-commission-on-race-and-ethnic-disparities/ summary-of-recommendations#contents (accessed 12 May 2022).

Department for Education (DfE) (2013) *National curriculum.* www.gov.uk/government/collections/national-curriculum

Ethnicity-facts-figures.service.gov.uk (2019) *School teacher workforce.* [online] www.ethnicity-facts-figures.service.gov.uk/workforce-and-business/workforce-diversity/school-teacher-workforce/ latest#by-ethnicity-and-gender-headteachers-only&gt (accessed 12 May 2022).

Explore-education-statistics.service.gov.uk (2022) *Permanent exclusions and suspensions in England, academic year 2020/21.* [online] https://explore-education-statistics.service.gov.uk/find-statistics/ permanent-and-fixed-period-exclusions-in-england&gt (accessed 10 May 2022).

Big questions

- Has the term BAME helped or hindered you when thinking about diversity in the curriculum?
- What dichotomies exist between the experiences of your students from Global Majority groups?
- Who is foregrounded as 'the other' in your curriculum? And what are the implications of this for your students?

12

Bouncer or Fetish

Kemi

The first school I worked in after I graduated university was my first experience of my skin colour being used for the role. I was very naive and didn't know what to say or do when the headteacher said 'you'll be good for the Black students, you'll know how to deal with them'. My second encounter was a few years later when I was told 'You're sassy and you can handle the kids we have here'. I've also had friends who work in various schools in and around London that were pushed, encouraged or only supported to go into roles where they could use their 'sass' or their physical build to help them deal with students exhibiting challenging behaviour. I don't consider myself to be sassy. As a professional, I conduct myself as such in the workplace, around my colleagues and students. But it was interesting that it was during my interview at both schools that I was told I'd be good for Black students and could use my 'sass'. They hadn't even seen me in the role yet on a day-to-day basis. Moreover, I had to question why I'd only be good for the Black students. How about all the other races and ethnicities – could they not benefit from having a Black woman teach them as well? I still get a raised eyebrow when I tell people I am a science teacher. There's this shock on their face and sometimes I'm met with 'I didn't think you'd be teaching such an academic subject; you must be really smart', and I reply 'Did you think I wasn't smart?' followed by an awkward laugh.

The Black body is used as a commodity in schools where those at the top feel it will be beneficial. In my experience, Black teachers have always been the 'go to' when it comes to managing behaviour, but we are so much more than bouncers. Our minds are filled with knowledge and intellect that we know can change the face of education.

Gradi Tomene – Does Black matter? My personal experience

Gradi Tomene is an assistant headteacher in a London secondary school, teaching for over 10 years, with over 15 years of experience working with young people. Gradi believes he was called into teaching by God, and that teaching is not just a job, but a vocation, one that he feels honoured to be a part of. His aim is to help young people develop and to advocate for those who look like him.

In comparison to white teachers, there are a smaller number of Black teachers in education, and this places us in a unique position. There are risks of negative experiences, whether intentional or unintentional due to ignorance, where Black teachers may mainly be used for their physique. But there are also opportunities for progress, where our unique experiences can support change and impact the lives of those who need it most. I have luckily experienced the latter, where I have always been approached based on my knowledge and areas of expertise – where I have been respected for the level of impact I bring, rather than the colour of the skin I am in. But, in saying this, I was once asked to cover PE lessons, due to 'looking in shape, like I go to the gym', which I certainly took as a compliment, knowing the positive relationship I had with my colleague.

Funnily enough, the comments have not stopped there, as I have received compliments, flattery and the odd awkward comment regarding my natural appearance and dress sense, but thankfully none that I have felt related directly to my Black skin. At times, I have had people compare me to Black celebrities in order to flatter me, but none done in an offensive way, although offence can easily be felt in these situations when those making the comments aren't aware of deep-rooted issues. These comments leave a mark, whether it is assuming Black staff are related because they share the same amount of melanin, questioning one's hair – its texture and style, or most annoyingly, negatively commenting on our cultural food. These types of comments negatively affect one's experience and feelings towards the workplace. What can be most upsetting about these comments is when those making them are aware of the possible offences and cultural issues. In these circumstances, my advice is to always speak up and use this as a teaching moment before needing to escalate it to HR.

Stereotypes and prejudice have an affect on all people and heavily influence how they see themselves and how others see them. Black pupils are commonly stereotyped as being loud and aggressive, which affects how they relate to teachers, authority figures and members of the public. These things can follow one into adulthood where Black people are, at times, afraid to speak up, and suppress their emotions, in order to not be seen as the 'angry Black woman/man'. The disheartening thing is that stereotypes are believed and followed rather than questioned. In these instances, not all Black pupils are loud, and for those who are, it can commonly be their way of expressing themselves, a likely learned behaviour from their household and upbringing – myself being of African heritage, it was not uncommon to be in a loud and loving home, or to witness family members shouting and laughing as they discussed politics, sports or played a simple game of Uno (Monopoly can also end friendships, ha ha). But sometimes, our pupils are loud because they feel unheard and desire to speak up; this isn't isolated to Black skin, but to all who struggle to be heard or to regulate their emotions.

I've witnessed occasions where Black children are described as aggressive and confrontational, when it is in fact frustration; frustration due to not being understood, frustration expressed through their communication, frustration of the situation that may have caused them to be in trouble. It is for us as professionals to be empathetic, where possible, and to aim to understand in order to resolve the matter, rather than being the cause of escalation and the further spreading of such horrible stereotypes. It is for this reason that I believe Black people working in behaviour roles can be a powerful thing, as long as we are not limited solely to those roles. I see the benefits of Black people being in behavioural roles; our experiences, upbringing and culture provide us with the tools necessary to support pupils with challenging behaviour, celebrate those with outstanding behaviour and train staff to be able to better work with these pupils. Although I am aware of Black teachers in teaching and learning roles, it is a small number compared to our non-Black counterparts, but then neither are there great numbers of Black teachers in education as a whole. We do need more Black teachers following the academic side and not just the pastoral. Our excellent work in behaviour management not only pigeonholes us into this one area, but unfortunately also hinders us from stepping out in order to explore more pedagogical expertise.

Ultimately, my experience in teaching, as a Black teacher, has been positive. I attribute this to the amazing school I work in that welcomed me and worked with me. This school, as well as its great leaders, have encouraged, trained and provided opportunities for growth and progression. As a minority leader and as a Black man, it is impressed upon me to be a representative of my people, to look out for those who look like me and to be a support for anyone who needs it. I am not biassed to a particular race, gender or group, and I am empathetic to all, but I do not hide my deep understanding of my people and the challenges that Black pupils face – it is for me to speak up on their behalf and to advocate when and where I can. It can be unfortunate that, at times, we Black teachers feel as though we need to take up such a heavy responsibility, but this is a privilege (just think back to the teachers who were there for you when you needed them the most). I am always honoured when parents of Black pupils, especially African parents, recognise me as one of their own and ask me to take their children under my wing, look out for them and treat them as my own kin. I am well aware that this is the parents' way of asking for help and their way of expressing their trust in me as a professional and as their child's teacher.

Teaching is a vocation, an honour, and I look forward to the rest of my journey, to what I hope to be a long and successful career. I certainly hope to make a difference and an impact.

Toby Williams – You're actually quite smart!

Often pigeonholed as the assertive enforcer, my pedagogy and technical knowledge felt overlooked. This is a teaching-specific extension of the comment 'You're actually quite smart!' and clearly a result of the perpetual stereotyping experienced by Black teachers. I would often be lauded for my behaviour management and physicality, despite not considering them my greatest strength, a point of constant frustration.

The irony is that Black male teachers, especially, are considered 'excellent role models and are in great demand' (Martino and Rezai-Rashti, 2012), yet we have our value predominantly attached to our physicality and disciplinarianism. I would be the one called upon to restrain the big, scary, violent Black boy, but never the one called to provide intricate academic input. This is the idea discussed by Callender (2018) that we are the 'antidotes to issues facing Black boys', seemingly reducing these issues to poor behaviour, aggression and disruption. This ideology is not limited to schools and teaching, however. Even in sports, research shows that Black players are often regarded for their physicality, whereas their white counterparts are praised for their psychological characteristics (McCarthy and Jones, 1997). Our 'big' 'brutish' bodies gain recognition, while our technical and intellectual capabilities are often unrecognised. Research by Billings (2004) analysed 162 hours of Black and white quarterbacks in collegiate and professional games and the 3,800 dés-ci-tors used for them. The research found that Black players were still characterised as succeeding because of athletic skill, whereas their white counterparts were depicted as failing because of their lack of innate ability.

This racial stereotyping extends to professional settings too. Professionalism is fundamentally a white-centric concept, leaving Black professionals often stereotyped as unprofessional. Looking at this within the context of the misrepresentation of Black skill, I am sure that many Black professionals anecdotally give an account of being incorrectly pigeonholed and seemingly being unable to shake these misrepresentations, modifying our behaviour in an attempt to make our professional lives easier. As a young Black leader, I became hyperaware that my credibility was inextricably linked to others' perception of me within the confines of white professionalism.

Consequently, I, as well as many other Black people, may then utilise a range of behavioural masking strategies in order to exist peacefully, secure progression and present positively within the workplace. Research (McCluney et al., 2021) has showed that Black professionals are perceived by white people as more professional if they engage in behaviours such as wearing a neutral hairstyle, adjusting speech and adjusting name. Although these strategies may increase the professional reputation of Black individuals, they reinforce white professional standards and incur a psychological cost on the person using them.

In line with research conducted by Sinclair and Kunda (1999), as professionals, we can activate these existing stereotypes by being put into contexts where we are assumed to be effective (such as intervening physically in a student altercation) and handling the difficult context successfully. This does nothing, however, for an accurate representation of the skills that are not aligned with our easily-activated stereotypes. As we would not be trusted to be put into these contexts, we would not be able to demonstrate skill in these areas.

This misrepresentation of my abilities I found exceptionally frustrating. I was frequently told that I was the strong role model that the boys needed, but what qualities did they want me to instil? The potential for physicality but actively choosing to use it for 'good'? Or my innovation, technical ability and drive for excellence? It has certainly felt like the former on numerous occasions, especially when my more technical contributions were dismissed or given noticeably less credence than others.

The contradiction between what I recognised to be my assets and what others perceived them to be, challenged my self-worth as a professional. Pabon (2016) talks about Black teachers being 'conceptualised as Black Supermen [but] are under supported and being pushed out of the very schools that claim to need them so much'. This eventually led me to have a teaching identity crisis. I felt like there was a monolithic view of what Black teachers were seen to be able to offer, and I would often wonder if these stereotypes were in fact correct. I had conversations with peers in similar situations and realised that the issue was way bigger than me just speaking out to challenge these ideologies.

I decided to take an introspective approach; objective awareness of my own skill set and areas to improve would take away the power of others' often skewed perceptions of me and my practice. Of course, external input is valuable when bettering practice, but attaching my worth to it was having a detrimental effect. This line of thought led me to reconsider my perception of healthy development. Where before I would place more emphasis on external feedback and judgement, I decided that it would factor, but I primarily would need to have an adept ability to self-reflect and accurately analyse my own abilities and areas for development.

Finding a role outside of teaching, where I am given space to demonstrate my wide skill set and find a use for my finer skills, reinforced what I had always known: I was more than a bouncer.

References

Billings, A.C. (2004) Depicting the quarterback in black and white: A content analysis of college and professional football broadcast commentary. *Howard Journal of Communications*, 15(4), 201–210.

Callender, C. (2018) Needles in a haystack: An exploratory study of Black male teachers in England. *Management in Education*, 32(4), 167–175.

Martino, W. and Rezai-Rashti, G. (2012) *Gender, race, and the politics of role modelling: The influence of male teachers*. London: Routledge.

McCarthy, D. and Jones, R.L. (1997) Speed, aggression, strength, and tactical naivete: The portrayal of the Black soccer player on television. *Journal of Sport and Social Issues*, 21(4), 348–362.

McCluney, C.L., Durkee, M.I., Smith II, R.E., Robotham, K.J. and Lee, S.S.L. (2021) To be, or not to be… Black: The effects of racial codeswitching on perceived professionalism in the workplace. *Journal of Experimental Social Psychology*, 97, 104199.

Pabon, A. (2016) Waiting for Black superman: A look at a problematic assumption. *Urban Education*, 51(8), 915–939.

Sinclair, L. and Kunda, Z. (1999) Reactions to a Black professional: Motivated inhibition and activation of conflicting stereotypes. *Journal of Personality and Social Psychology*, 77(5), 885.

Big questions

- How objectively based on fact are judgements that you make on others' practice?
- What do you often hear are your strengths and weaknesses professionally?
- How well do they match with your reflections on your own practice?

13

Black Leaders

Caren – Black leaders in education: Shattering the silence, shaping the future

Education is often heralded as the great equaliser, a pathway to social mobility and a brighter future. However, for Black students, this promise can be dimmed by systemic inequities and a lack of representation in leadership positions. Black leaders in education play a crucial role in dismantling these barriers, fostering a sense of belonging and ensuring all students have the opportunity to thrive.

One of the key strengths of Black leadership lies in its understanding of the unique challenges faced by Black students and families, particularly those from immigrant backgrounds. Many Black immigrant families come from educational systems with vastly different structures and expectations. Navigating a new educational landscape, sometimes with limited English proficiency, can be daunting for both parents and children (Fordham, 1996). Black leaders, who may share similar experiences or cultural backgrounds, can bridge this gap. They can create culturally responsive classrooms and support systems that acknowledge the students' lived experiences and affirm their identities (Ladson-Billings, 1995).

Furthermore, Black leaders can serve as powerful role models, shattering the unspoken rules that often permeate educational spaces. These unspoken rules, the unwritten expectations of behaviour and cultural norms, can disadvantage Black students. A Black headteacher, leader or teacher challenges the implicit bias that may exist within the school, demonstrating that success is attainable, regardless of race or background (Ferguson, 2001). This positive representation fosters a sense of self-efficacy among Black students, encouraging them to pursue academic excellence and leadership roles themselves (Carter, 2003). In Jeffrey Boakye's book *I Heard What You Said* (2022), he tells the tale of his amazing English teacher Mr Seba, a Ugandan teacher who fostered a love of literature in him and inspired him to study it all the way through to university, eventually becoming a teacher himself and writing numerous books. This is the power of representation.

Black leadership also benefits all students by fostering a more inclusive and equitable learning environment. By creating a curriculum that acknowledges the contributions of Black people throughout history and celebrates Black culture, Black leaders ensure a richer educational experience for everyone. This exposure combats historical inaccuracies and promotes empathy and understanding among students of all backgrounds (Howard, 2006).

The impact of Black leaders extends beyond the classroom walls. They advocate for policies and resources that address the specific needs of Black students and their families. Black leaders can ensure that schools are adequately funded, have culturally competent staff development programmes, and cultivate strong partnerships with Black communities (Darling-Hammond, 2010). This collaborative approach empowers Black families to participate actively in their children's education, fostering a sense of agency and shared responsibility for student success.

However, the path to leadership is not without obstacles. Black educators often face a glass ceiling, encountering racial bias and limited opportunities for advancement and career progression (Gutiérrez, 2004). Addressing this underrepresentation requires a multi-pronged approach. Mentorship programmes can support and guide aspiring Black leaders, while schools and MATs must implement hiring practices that value diversity and lived experiences.

In a nutshell, Black leadership in education is not simply about filling a quota. It's also about creating a space where all students, regardless of race or background, feel valued, empowered and equipped to reach their full potential. Black leaders break down cultural barriers, shatter unspoken rules and advocate for a more equitable educational system. By investing in and nurturing Black leadership, we pave the way for a brighter future, not just for Black students, but for all.

References

Boakye, J. (2022) *I heard what you said: A Black teacher, a white system.* London: Pan Macmillan.

Carter, K. (2003*) The contradictions of Black college leadership: Power, race, and the struggle for equity.* Sterling, VA: Stylus Publishing.

Darling-Hammond, L. (2010) *The flat world and education: How America's commitment to equity will determine our future.* New York, NY: Teachers College Press.

Ferguson, A.A. (2001) *Black educators in white schools: Desegregation's forgotten heroes.* New York, NY: Teachers College Press.

Fordham, S. (1996) *Black parents speak out: The education of our children in the context of social change*. New York, NY: Routledge.

Gutiérrez, R. (2004) The effects of race and social class on becoming a teacher. *American Educational Research Journal*, 41(3), 647–674.

Howard, G.R. (2006) *We can't teach what we don't know: White teachers, Black students*. New York, NY: Teachers College Press.

Ladson-Billings, G. (1995) Culturally relevant teaching, anti-racism, and the development of democratic citizens. *The Teachers College Record*, 97(1), 115–129.

Kemi – Imposter syndrome is real

Definition: the persistent inability to believe that one's success is deserved or has been legitimately achieved as a result of one's own efforts or skills.

The jump from middle leadership to senior leadership is no joke. Even though I had prepared for it in different ways over the years – I had coaching and mentoring, I kept a portfolio of different initiatives I've led on, implemented and the impact they had on students and as a whole school – I just couldn't fathom being a senior leader now that I was in the role. I had the 'I made it' moment and then I was hit with fear: will I succeed? Will I have a good impact on students, the team I manage, and whole-school improvement? Am I the right person for the role?

I have never questioned myself as much as I did since becoming an assistant headteacher. I have questioned my abilities and everything that had all led me to this point.

Getting to senior leadership wasn't an easy journey. I received a lot of rejections when applying for roles and even when I was shortlisted for interviews, I had headteachers that would say 'You're knowledgeable, you have the experience and you answered our questions well as well as the in-tray tasks, but…' The 'but' would make my heart sink followed by an internal eye roll. 'But' made me think I wasn't good enough, qualified enough. 'But' would stop me in my tracks and demotivate me. The worst part was, on a few occasions, 'but' would be followed by 'we don't think you'll be the right fit for our school'. When you're being interviewed by an all-white panel, I'm sure we can all guess why I wouldn't be the right fit. As a Black woman, I'd stick out like a sore thumb. In one school I worked in, one senior leader said parents wanted to see senior leaders who looked 'British', hence why there were no Black people on the senior leadership team. I guess being Black British wasn't British enough.

What I thought was a glass ceiling was more like a concrete roof, so it was harder to break through. Once I got the opportunity to be an assistant headteacher, I was excited and ready to go. I was ready to show what I could bring to the table as I had done many times before. I was ready to learn, grow and develop as a senior leader. Maybe this was what would make me stay in teaching for longer.

Being a leader taught me, more than ever, the importance of protecting my peace and wellbeing. I remember receiving hurtful comments from staff in an envelope (all typed and anonymous of course) within the first few weeks of term. I was also told that some colleagues did not feel comfortable coming to my office, because too many Black members of staff would be in there. I was told some people didn't like being managed by a Black woman. The things I heard I took with a pinch of salt, because 'he said, she said' was something I tried not to dwell on. I tried to have tough skin, but at times, it wasn't tough enough. The mistake I made was not raising it and trying to handle it alone because the hurtful, anonymous comments stung and left a bad taste in my mouth. Call me crazy, but I RAGd the comments after receiving advice from another colleague on what to do; what was mean, hurtful and personal was Red and thrown in the bin (in the words of J. Hus, 'they can't touch my spirit'). What I could use as an area of development was Amber, and comments that weren't hurtful and had something positive in them somewhere, I RAGd as Green.

I realised very early on that my first year as a senior leader was going to be difficult. I had also set standards for myself which were high and I didn't want to mess up. In fact, I was so focused on not messing up because I didn't want to ruin it for the next Black person who'd be joining SLT. I put myself under a ridiculous amount of internal pressure on top of the pressure I was already feeling externally. I didn't want to fail or mess up as the *only* Black person on SLT. I had to remind myself that I applied for the role and interviewed just like every other candidate, so I shouldn't have doubted myself. The role wasn't handed to me. It wasn't nepotism. It was nine years in the making of: training, teaching, learning, professional development, coaching, mentoring, impact evidence collating, applying, interviewing and rejections, before this opportunity came about.

I am grateful to all the leaders who spoke to me and gave me advice before I entered my leadership role and whilst in the role, as they prepared me on what to expect and what I can and should do differently from what they experienced, the lessons they learned and what they passed on to me. It is important that we always lead with integrity and that we pass the baton on or the ladder down to those who are coming after us, as they will also need support to thrive and succeed as leaders.

Evelyn Forde MBE – Taking a seat at the table

Evelyn Forde MBE is a successful headteacher, winner of the TES HT of the Year award and the first Black female president of ASCL which represents over 24,000 members. Evelyn was the founding Chair of ASCL's Ethnic Diversity Network and is a strong advocate for aspiring Black leaders in education.

I am headteacher of Copthall School in Mill Hill, London and also the President of the Association of School and College Leaders (ASCL). I am immensely proud and humbled to hold such prestigious roles in the education sector, and I recognise that I am a role model for others and am certainly holding the door open so others can follow.

When I decided to go into senior leadership, I had no idea it would be such a challenge. After all, I had a degree from a Russell Group university, followed by a PGCE from the prestigious Institute of Education. But a challenge it was – I attended over 20 deputy headteacher (DHT) interviews, getting down to the final two for most of them, only to be told that I wasn't the right fit or the panel were not sure how the community would relate to me. This feedback remained with me and that is why I use my privileged positions to highlight the barriers faced by people of colour and do everything I can to support and encourage those who are on their leadership journey because I know they are encountering the same feedback that I did. This can knock your confidence to such an extent that it is easier to give up. However, with the emergence of grassroots groups like Aspiring Heads, WomenEd and BAMEed, more people are feeling encouraged to keep on going.

I am aware that unconscious bias plays a huge part in the lack of leadership appointments and, whilst some schools are doing great work in this area, until governing bodies and Trust leaders truly believe that there is talent in people of colour and that having diverse representation means so much to our young people and their families, that glass ceiling will not shift. The 3% figure of BAME headteachers is woeful and definitely not representative of most school communities, and I am truly saddened that even over time that figure is only marginally shifting. Our young people need to see people that look like them as do our staff and families, so as I enter my presidential year with ASCL I have chosen the theme of Empowering Leadership as a way to work with others to bring about that leadership change.

2020 was an immense year for me – I won TES Headteacher of the Year and I was awarded an MBE for services to education, both of which have given me the confidence to be in a room when I am the only Black face and to represent. I feel an additional pressure sometimes that I can't get things wrong but I also know that we need to be in the room, we need to be at the table and the head of the table at that, so I am OK with the pressure because I know that I inspire others who someday soon will take over the baton and continue to elevate the voices of our communities.

Adrian McLean – Leading whilst Black

Adrian is a current executive leader and former headteacher, who knows first hand the pressures and challenges facing Black people in leadership positions, both in and outside of the education sector. Adrian is an ambassador of Character Education, a trustee of Governors for Schools, and an advisory board member for ImpactED and Reach Out 2 Kids.

The stark reality of the numbers of Black male educators, especially those in senior leadership positions, is one that is well documented. Having been a head-teacher – now an executive leader of a multi-academy trust – I am somewhat of a unicorn. There are not many who have my characteristics and hold such positions of influence in education!

The glass ceiling is very real, one that 'could' have stalled/ended my career out of frustration if I had let it. My own self-belief, resilience and relentless drive to succeed against the odds have meant I have achieved a seat at the table. However, that is not enough. I am often the only Black face in the room and I 'feel' the eyes of judgement from the white, middle-class (mostly) men, who have a very different life experience to mine. Their collective experience often is very alien to mine and the alternate viewpoint I offer. Microaggressions, discrediting and dismissive judgement of 'what value to the discussions and decisions does this guy add?' are made. It used to intimidate me… knowing that my performance would be a yardstick for those who followed. I initially felt like an imposter, that I did not belong and I would be found out. Naturally, I wanted to blend in, not rock the boat. However, that is not my character, I have never been that way. My authentic self and core values would not allow it! After all, that is what got me to this point.

A conversation with my grandfather reminded me that all of these people are not me, and they cannot bring what I bring to the table. That pep talk was all I needed to fortify my thinking and be my unapologetic, authentic self as a leader. This has often made things difficult, as I have had to choose between continuing in roles and compromising my values.

The discrimination I faced in attempts to attain headship simply made me more determined to break through the glass ceiling. Having a white British sounding name often helped get me through the initial application sort process… in some cases, their whole demeanour changed when meeting me in person! Post-interview process, there was often no constructive feedback: 'not the right fit', 'we wanted someone with more experience' or my favourite – 'it was very close between you and the successful candidate, however they answered *a* question in the final interview better than you'. This was despite ranking first in all other aspects of the process.

At no point have I been deterred from pushing on further, as painful as it has been to repeatedly put myself through the process of rejection. History has taught us all that changing the status quo is full of trials and tribulations, a journey I am fully committed to embracing; frustrations and all. My role is to continue opening doors, holding them open for others who look like me to follow through.

Big questions

- What are your core values? Are you willing to go against them to progress?
- Do you have a coach/mentor to help you navigate some of the barriers you face along your journey?
- What allies and coalitions can you build to be positive advocates for you?

Audrey Pantelis – The hurdles and highlights of being Black in school leadership

Audrey's career in education as teacher, middle leader, senior leader and head of school in both mainstream and special educational needs spans over 32 years. She gained her National Professional Qualification in Headship (NPQH) in 2007. She was the founding head of a free special school in northwest London where she led the school through its first Ofsted inspection, and it gained a 'Good with outstanding features' judgement. Audrey is an accredited Resilient Leaders Elements leadership coach and C-Me colour profiling accreditor. She works with schools and organisations in developing and implementing positive, systemic changes with regard to racial diversity and strategic inclusive practices.

One morning, in March 2005, I made a decision. After teaching in mainstream secondary schools as a music teacher, head of department and head of faculty (performing arts), I recognised that I wanted to do more. I wanted to have the opportunity to positively impact the life chances of the next generation. At the time, I did not think too deeply about race, but I was aware that there weren't many people that looked like me doing 'the top job'. Still, undeterred, I set out to achieve my new goal. I thought that it would be straightforward – I would apply, get interviewed and get a job. No. That would have been too easy.

The first challenge was to move from middle leadership to senior leadership. This is hard for all applicants generally, as you move from a subject-specific to a whole-school perspective. The application process was difficult for the reasons listed but as a Black educator there is the unspoken factor of 'fit'. If you are looking at a school where the student cohort is diverse, but the staffing cohort is not, how does that work? Factors that prospective Black leaders must consider include:

- How supported would a Black candidate be within their role?
- What opportunities are there for Black candidates to further their leadership career?
- Are there any external networking groups that a Black candidate can access?

These factors were not apparent to me at the time, but they are definitely factors that I would insist upon now for all prospective candidates. 'Fit' is a big factor regarding inclusion and belonging and a major factor in the attrition rate regarding senior leadership for Black leaders. I experienced some real barriers where my experience would have added value, but a lack of vision and a lack of understanding about the benefits of recruiting Black candidates were prominent and exercised regularly. The barriers included:

- demographics
- culture
- prejudice.

Now, don't get me wrong; I am all about the best person for the job. We need the best person for the job to improve the life chances of the children and young people that we serve, so there's *no* room for error. In an ideal world, meritocracy rules and, at the time, I believed this to be true and I very much followed this idea as I applied for post after post, but I observed middle leaders with *less* experience than me gaining senior positions.

Prospective Black candidates for senior leadership roles are often overqualified because we have been told to gain experience – and from personal experience – to ensure that we are not rejected – we 'Prove-It-Again' (Williams and Dempsey, 2014). Working harder than our peers to do exactly the same job ... time after time after time. Let's unpack the barriers that were mentioned earlier.

Demographics

This may include the area/catchment that the school is placed in or, thinking bigger picture, the geographic area where there is a lack of diverse people.

As a result, and I must add that in general it is not always malicious, it can be more difficult to navigate your way around an area that doesn't have any or many people that look like you. Interview panels cannot always see past this factor. Equally, as a candidate you may decide that this isn't an area that you feel psychologically safe within. This factor may become apparent during the interview process.

Culture

This doesn't always relate to you as the candidate, but the culture of the school. Maybe it is a school that has a strong 'pub' culture which you do not share. Or maybe you have a strong social culture that isn't shared with your colleagues, and this is something that is important to you? It may be that there are other aspects of the culture that don't sit well with you that you would be expected to accept. We all want to feel psychologically safe – and seeing an organisation that behaves in a way that enables us to feel safe is part of the 'unseen checklist' that we mentally go through.

Prejudice

It's a well tried-and-tested barrier but it's the most frequent one that is presented by one or more members of any interviewing panel. It can be overt or covert, but it is there. Panels can decide whether you are going to 'fit in' based on the little that they know about you – which is their prerogative – but when you can do the job on paper – which is why you were shortlisted – why does the process stop?

These challenges are evident in a variety of ways and are usually not part of any debrief that you will ever receive. This is an internal debrief that happens and can deter you from completing another application form. But you do – and you can make it into senior leadership!

Once you are 'in', it's like anything that you do – you need to work at it, but being the only Black face in the room means that you are more conspicuous. There is more pressure that you didn't ask for. Sometimes you will have to laugh at jokes. Sometimes you won't and will subsequently be labelled 'touchy'. Sometimes you will have to explain why the phrase that has been used is incorrect. It's a lot. This is where an external networking group for Black professionals is desirable and something to be sought out. The major leadership unions, i.e. the National Association of Head Teachers (NAHT) and the Association of School and College Leaders (ASCL), have recently developed networking groups for Black leaders but there are other independent groups that can support Black senior leaders. They do an excellent job – speaking on issues that are pertinent to leaders like us.

Moving from middle leadership to senior leadership is a hard transition generally. Black leaders have, from my own experience, several hurdles to negotiate and manage – and that is just to get the role! Prejudices, experiences, opportunities – these all conspire against us, but there is so much that we bring to any school – vibrancy, creativity, positivity – the list is endless! One of the most important things that we do bring is representation.

Children and young people who look like us, see adults who look like them in leadership positions, which enables them to aspire to do the same – not necessarily just in education but in all professions that they choose to lean into. We bring life into all that we do – and this should be embraced, nurtured and valued.

Reference

Williams, J.C. and Dempsey, R. (2014) *What works for women at work: Four patterns working women need to know.* NYU Press.

Paige Griffin – My leadership journey and the power of Black influences

Paige Griffin is a mum and educator with over 10 years' experience of working in a range of schools. She is a highly passionate woman, especially in regards to SEND and encouraging Black educators into leadership. Paige currently works as a SEND educational consultant and aspires to promote inclusion and equal opportunities for all.

Being in education for 10 years has exposed me to many experiences that I want to share to encourage more Black leaders in schools. I hope I can motivate you to push yourself out of your comfort zone to reach your dreams.

My journey started as a teaching assistant, but I soon realised that I wanted to be at the front teaching and applied to do my PGCE. What an intense year full of tears, joys and late nights planning whilst writing essays! I completed my PGCE and secured a job in a school with predominantly Black students and staff.

Leadership was not something I thought I would achieve for a long time or aspired to; I felt I had a lot to learn in regards to teaching first. I was amazed to have a senior leadership team made up of mainly Black female leaders; I felt immensely supported and encouraged by them. I have always been a very quiet and private person, and I have never been one to broadcast my successes, although this was being done for me constantly by my leadership team. I remember being referred to as a future leader and future headteacher but could never see what they saw in me. They continued to champion and push me to reach my full potential.

I soon found myself as a middle leader and was not sure how I managed to get myself in this position. I was an outstanding teacher, but was lacking the confidence in leading others. I found this new role challenging at times but exciting and was keen to share my expertise to help others and wanted to learn how to do this effectively. On reflection, I was not a confident leader at this point and was most likely experiencing imposter syndrome. I was quite reserved in meetings and did not challenge members of staff when I could have done, but thankfully I had a supportive team around me.

I had taught Year 5 for three years consecutively and felt I had reached a point where I wanted to see if I could thrive elsewhere and began looking for jobs in new schools. My headteacher was keen for me to stay and asked what my goals and interests were; without hesitation, I mentioned my passion for SEN and she instantly encouraged and supported me onto the SENCO qualification course.

I began the course and also taught Year 6 for the first time. I felt overwhelmed and scared, but I had the most amazing Year 6 team who helped me through one of the toughest years of my career. Doing a Master's course whilst trying to teach a challenging Year 6 class, what pressure! Things changed as my headteacher retired and very quickly the Black leadership team who were inspiring and motivating me had disappeared completely and I was left having to prove myself.

The following year, I was a SENCO whilst teaching and mentoring a student teacher. The range of responsibilities was challenging as I was unable to do each role to a high standard. I approached the headteacher and asked for more time away from class to focus on the SENCO role as promised, but this was shut down. I also wanted her to create a leadership role for me and to have a pay increment. I displayed an evidence folder of my impact, progress and vision as part of my professional development meeting. This was shut down and I felt as though I was undeserving of this.

With encouragement from family, peers and colleagues, after six years at the only school I had taught at and had learnt so much from, I plucked up the courage to apply for an assistant headteacher role as a SENCO at a specialist school; they loved me and I got offered the job the same day. I felt so valued, appreciated and respected. It was just what I needed, and although I was now attending a school with an all-white senior leadership team, I felt empowered to be the only Black member of that leadership team.

I was accepted and felt part of a family, although my first uncomfortable experience as a leader was in an external meeting where I was the only young, Black person in the room. I felt invisible, out of place and as though I was perceived as an inexperienced person. I wish I had been prepared for this experience in some way – if I could go back, I would have improved my posture to appear confident, introduced myself instantly and contributed more to the session.

Another Black teacher joined the leadership team at my school, and I felt relieved to not be the only one. As a leader, I felt a sense of pressure being the only Black female leader, as my Black colleagues would confide in me and share concerns. I felt I was in the middle, at times being pulled and pressured from both ends, but also felt happy that I was able to relate to my Black colleagues in ways that other leaders could not. I would advise future leaders to set expectations from day one and to be mindful when establishing relationships; not to become too friendly but to also appear as approachable and assertive.

I have learnt that Black educators are not presented with routes into leadership; they are not hidden but also not actively presented to us. What I would suggest is for more Black educators to push and find ways into leadership. What are your strengths? What are you passionate about? Once you have established this, what opportunities can you take or ask for around these? You need to establish a goal and establish the steps to get there; if unsure, find a mentor or coach to guide you.

I was very fortunate to have leaders and a supportive network inspiring and pushing me to progress, but for those that don't have that you need to find your network and the drive to push yourself to achieve more. There is no limit for us as Black leaders, but unfortunately it may be more difficult for us and you may have to work harder at times to prove just how amazing you are. Is there someone doing a role you are interested in? How can you shadow, observe and learn from them?

When faced with challenges in leadership, always be professional and think before you speak because how and what you say can be used against you; it is unfair but it is something to be aware of. Follow up conversations and agreements with an email so that you have a paper trail. If you feel unhappy to the point that it is affecting your happiness or mental health, consider moving on; there are children everywhere who need you and you will maintain real friendships. If you are not appreciated and are not being given what you deserve, then find somewhere else who will appreciate you. The sky is really the limit; we must continue to empower each other and see more Black leaders in schools. It is tough like all things worthwhile, but it is possible.

Toby Williams – Learning to lead the way

From a young age, I had been around leadership positions, learning and developing my understanding of leadership and what it meant. I was privileged enough to see that leadership was about facilitating the development of your team, coordinating a team of individuals toward an aligned goal and recognising individuals for their strengths and areas for development. I found myself naturally assuming leadership roles from sports to job roles. My experience of leadership was not wholly positive, nor was the journey there, but important to me was the 'why' when encountering obstacles. For me, impact on others and personal development were the driving force for my development into leadership.

The plight of Black professionals ascending to leadership is well covered anecdotally, however the experience when in these positions is significant, too. It requires guile, grit and strength. The dearth of faces like ours within leadership roles means that we are often at the vanguard when in these positions, restricting the potential for building and relying upon peer-support networks. I experienced a mixture of the problems I faced when working toward leadership and new leadership-specific issues. Overcoming white-centric standards of professionalism and stereotypes continued, but I had the new challenges of building credibility and negotiating nuanced peer and direct-report relationships.

We often theorise that our way of shattering the glass ceiling for Black professionals in leadership is to get into the room to scaffold the way in for others. However, it can be exceptionally frustrating when you feel as if you had been invited into the room to contribute, but then realise otherwise. At times, it has felt as if my expertise and unique perspective were often overlooked, eliciting feelings that I was invited to solely be the face in the room. This is a disheartening conclusion to draw after tirelessly working to earn my seat at the table.

Black professionals often cite having to work twice as hard as their counterparts to get the same recognition. In research by Korn Ferry (2019), just under 60% of the Black executives at Fortune 500 companies felt that they had to work twice as hard and achieve twice as much to be recognised the same as their peers, all whilst being assigned complex projects that no others would have taken on. The underrepresentation of Black educators in leadership positions within schools has been often characterised by research as a product of institutional racism (Bush, 2011; Shepard, 2011). To be honest, it is hard to dispute such an argument when research has shown that Black and minority ethnic (BAME) teachers have been less likely than their white counterparts to receive promotions into leadership positions (Powney et al., 2003). This is something I certainly can testify to as the often odd Black face in the room full of school leaders.

In some leadership contexts, I have found that I had to be an expert and outstanding in order to build any credibility whereas others appeared to be mediocre. I would often be seen as an unprofessional liability and too relaxed, with no appreciation for how problematic things were, or this reinforced negative stereotypes. However, I would, somewhat contradictorily, achieve excellent feedback from external sources for my areas of responsibility. With such an environment a test of my professional resilience and stamina, I would centre myself around my purpose for pursuing leadership – helping those that looked like me (future leaders and students alike) that were held back by the systems and structures that we were forced to abide by. Johnson (2017) discusses how trailblazing Black British headteachers from older generations shared more activist and community leader identities, whereas younger Black leaders were more focused on supporting the achievement of marginalised groups.

I would not claim that all of my leadership experiences have been negative, however. When I felt like I was trusted, safe and appreciated as a leader, I thrived and would eagerly bring diverse thought and innovation to the table. I found that leaders that came from a point of humility and had accepted that they would learn from their direct reports, too, got the best out of me. With these leaders, I would exist above survival mode and feel less risk-averse. They would inherently build a safe environment that would encourage me to access higher-level skills and accelerate my development.

It is reasonable to assert that the environment and culture that we are brought into makes or breaks the success of the Black leader, but it is our responsibility to recreate such an environment to facilitate the development of others. We unquestionably bring such value to leadership roles when given the opportunity, safety and trust. We are often driven by moral purpose with a cultural awareness (Johnson and Campbell-Stephens, 2010) that sets us apart. We represent ambition and success for all pupils but have an even greater impact on pupils that relate to us through our dual roles within the Black community and the educational establishment (Callender, 1995).

References

Bush, T. (2011) Succession planning in England: New leaders and new forms of leadership. *School Leadership & Management*, 31(3), 181–198.

Callender, C. (1995) A question of 'style': Black teachers and pupils in multi-ethnic schools. *Language and Education*, 9(3), 145–159.

Johnson, L. (2017) The lives and identities of UK Black and South Asian head teachers: Metaphors of leadership. *Educational Management Administration & Leadership*, 45(5), 842–862.

Johnson, L. and Campbell-Stephens, R. (2010) Investing in Diversity in London schools: Leadership preparation for Black and Global Majority educators. *Urban Education*, 45(6), 840–870.

Johnson, L. and Campbell-Stephens, R. (2013) Developing the next generation of Black and global majority leaders for London schools. *Journal of Educational Administration*, 1, 24–39.

Korn Ferry (2019) *The Black P&L leader.* www.kornferry.com/content/dam/
    kornferry/docs/pdfs/korn-ferry_theblack-pl-leader.pdf (accessed 1 August 2022).

Powney, J., Wilson, V., Hall, S., Davidson, J., Kirk, S., Edward, S. and Mirza, H.S.
    (2003) *Teachers' careers: The impact of age, disability, ethnicity, gender and
    sexual orientation.* London: Department for Education and Skills.

Shepard, L. (2011) Black male headteachers in England state schools number just
    30. *The Guardian*, 21 April. www.theguardian.com/education/2011/apr/21/
    black-male-headteachers-state-schools (accessed 21 April 2024).

Big questions

- What do you think a leader is?
- What is the culture that you wish to instil in your team?
- How can you build an environment that pulls others up into leadership?

14

Why We Need the Arts

Caren – The vital role of the arts in Black education: Identity, empowerment, and academic success

For all students, the arts are not merely an enrichment activity; they are an essential component of a well-rounded education. For Black students, Arts education provides a platform for cultural identity exploration, fosters critical thinking skills and empowers students to navigate a world that often presents limited narratives of Black excellence. The arts hold a significant place in Black education: highlighting its impact on students, teachers, families, and the overall educational experience.

One of the most crucial contributions of the arts in Black education is the fostering of a strong cultural identity. Black visual and musical art forms like jazz, blues, grime, Afrobeats, cubism and more are steeped in African diasporic traditions, which offer students a rich tapestry of heritage to connect with (The National Conference of Artists, n.d.). By engaging with these art forms, students gain a deeper understanding of their history, traditions, and the struggles and triumphs of past generations. This connection to their cultural roots empowers students with a sense of belonging and self-worth, which directly translates into increased academic motivation and achievement (Carter, 2003). Teachers play a vital role in this process by creating inclusive art spaces that celebrate Black culture and artists. They can curate curriculum materials that showcase the vast contributions of Black artists throughout history, allowing students to see themselves reflected in the artistic landscape. As a teacher, I have always championed the arts: from museum and gallery trips, to displaying art from around the world on my classroom walls.

Furthermore, the arts equip Black students with critical thinking skills that benefit them both inside and outside the classroom. Art forms like drama require students to analyse complex narratives, understand character motivations, and think creatively to solve problems. In music, students delve into music theory, notation, and performance techniques, fostering analytical thinking and problem-solving skills. These skills readily translate to other academic disciplines, enhancing students' ability to analyse texts, solve maths problems, and approach scientific inquiry with a critical lens (Eisner, 2002). Additionally, the arts encourage expression and open-mindedness, fostering empathy and intercultural dialogue. This is particularly important for Black students who may often encounter dominant narratives that fail to represent their experiences. Through artistic expression, students develop a voice and learn to articulate their perspectives with confidence. I remember the day I was introduced to a flute after years of the recorder. I felt like I had just discovered a new way to tell stories. I was very lucky in that my parents always supported extra-curricular pursuits in the arts and I left school being able to play the flute, cello and violin, as well as studying Art to A-Level. However, like most traditional African families, they weren't too keen on me turning these pursuits into a career! When I attend the opera, or visit a Lina Iris Viktor exhibition, my inner child cries at the lost opportunity of becoming an artist.

The benefits of arts education extend beyond the individual student. Teachers who integrate the arts into their curriculum create engaging learning environments that cater to diverse learning styles. Art projects provide a platform for kinaesthetic learners to shine, while visual learners can engage with information through images and presentations. Starters/Do Now activities based on paintings centuries old always go down well in the classroom and allow for a lively debate and discussion. This inclusive approach fosters a more positive and supportive classroom atmosphere, where all students feel valued and able to contribute (Walker, 2016).

For families, the arts can bridge the gap between home and school, fostering a sense of community and shared purpose. When schools prioritise arts education and involve families in artistic endeavours, a sense of collaboration and support is cultivated. Parents and caregivers love to witness their children thrive in creative spaces, performing and presenting 'what they have learned' and thereby fostering a deeper understanding of the importance of the arts in their children's holistic development. This collaborative approach empowers families to become active partners in their children's education, advocating for continued arts scheduling within the school system. Let us all champion the arts and encourage school to put on an annual panto, musical or performance. Let's attend and volunteer as stakeholders, supporting the often financially stretched Art, Drama and Music departments.

Despite budget cuts and time constraints, we must not let the arts become a peripheral aspect of Black education; they are an integral force for empowerment, self-discovery, and academic achievement. By integrating the arts into the wider school curriculum, educators create opportunities for Black students to connect with their heritage, develop critical thinking skills, and find their voice. Furthermore, the arts cultivate a more inclusive learning environment for all students and foster a sense of collaboration between school and family. Investing in arts education for Black students is not just about fostering creativity; it is about nurturing well-rounded individuals equipped with the tools to navigate the world and achieve their full potential.

References

Carter, K.C. (2003) The relationship between arts education and student achievement in ethnically diverse, urban school districts. *Urban Education*, 38(3), 263–279.

Eisner, E.W. (2002) What does it mean to say a school is 'arts-centered'? *Journal of Aesthetic Education*, 36(1), 31–44.

The National Conference of Artists (n.d.) *Why arts education for African American youth?* https://dc.blac.media/arts-culture/why-its-still-so-important-for-the-future-of-our-youth

Walker, L. (2016) *Why arts education matters for Black students*. Teach for America. https://wordinblack.com/2023/02/black-students-deserve-equitable-access-to-arts-education

Kemi – Rap music is educational

Growing up in a Nigerian household, the arts weren't seen as a serious way of making a living. My parents wanted us to enjoy our hobbies, but creative subjects were seen as leisurely activities. The only options for you were; law, medicine, accounting and engineering. Those were the top four. As I grew older and became a teacher, I saw how invaluable the arts were. I saw how students came alive in art studios and during their on-stage performances. I saw how the arts helped to shape and built confidence in young people as well as nurture their skills and talents. I also saw how some students were able to breathe and relax when they were painting, drawing, singing, dancing or acting, in comparison to when they were balancing equations or learning about titration. Creative subjects like music, art and drama do the following things:

- develop critical thinking
- develop verbal skills
- develop communication skills
- develop fine motor skills and visual-spatial processing
- encourage curiosity and boost imagination
- instil discipline
- strengthen memory
- help students to accept constructive criticism
- help students to express themselves in ways they wouldn't normally do
- help students to gain a better understanding of who they are
- allow students to think outside of the box
- enable students to see the beauty in different things around them
- promote innovation.

If the arts can do all of these things plus more, why do we not place as much emphasis on creative subjects as we do with academic subjects such as maths, English and science?

Yes, we have to teach the curriculum and as much as schools want to focus on wellbeing, they are still driven by grades and data. But imagine how much more we can get out of students in terms of engagement and participation in our lessons if we incorporate creativity and the arts. We could nurture their gifts and talents in our classrooms and personalise learning for them to ensure they make progress. During my training and NQT year rap music was used in my lessons to help students revise for assessments. I would allow students to get into teams and come up with a song or a rap to help them remember what they had learned. I knew it worked when one day as I was marking one of my students' end of year assessments, I noticed he had written out his rap in the top left-hand corner of his exam paper to help him remember which metals react with acid and oxygen. This student was one who struggled with 6-mark exam style questions and writing his ideas coherently, but for the first time, he got all 6 marks and I'll never forget the look on his face when I handed his paper back to him. Priceless.

When I worked in a PRU, I had two students who were so talented and loved drama, I gave them different responsibilities in my class and they were natural leaders who loved group activities. They also modelled what to do to their peers which also supported their learning. With the understanding I have now of the arts and how it helps the learning and development of children and young people, I hope moving forward, more of us will take the arts more seriously and see the importance of creative subjects in the curriculum.

Alessandro Babalola – Art reflects life reflects life reflects art

Alessandro Babalola is an Olivier award-winning actor, writer, director, musician and dramaturg of Nigerian descent, born and raised in East London. He studied acting at the Arts University of Bournemouth. He has performed in various short films including 'Samantha's Choice' which was selected for Cannes Film Festival in 2016. Alessandro has also done various London theatre productions and regional productions. In 2017 Alessandro Babalola landed 'FLESH & BONE' (Soho Theatre) with Unpolished Theatre company which won him an Olivier Award in 2019. His performance in 'FLESH & BONE' led to him being cast in season 3 of 'Top Boy' on Netflix; a performance that had him placed on Evening Standard's one to watch for 2020. Alessandro was then cast in another Netflix original called 'Cursed'. He was later cast in ITV's detective series 'Unforgotten' (2020), featured prominently in Guy Ritchie's 'Wrath Of Man' (2021) and Guy Ritchie's 'Ministry Of Ungentlemanly Warfare' (2024). Alessandro has written and directed four plays, is Artist in Residence at Soho Theatre, on the board for Soho Theatre and is the Co Chair of the Soho Theatre Walthamstow board.

As children, we are all far more connected to our creative core than we are as adults. As children, we have a natural and intuitive capacity for creativity that is almost boundless. The imagination of a child is essentially limitless, which is why at a particular age: children are able to believe anything you tell them. They do not spend time internally critiquing or judging; rather they accept what is being offered and go with it. It is this same quality that allows a child to play games with such adventurous and impossible storylines, enjoy wacky nonsensical cartoons or tell lies that are not limited by the constraints of possibility. I remember playing games in which the stairs in my childhood home were a volcano or Mount Everest in *Mission Impossible*. I fondly remember creating intergalactic battles for the universe using everything from my favourite bedroom toys to old cutlery and broken pens. In my adult profession as an actor, writer and director I draw on the same parts of my mind that were constantly being employed during childhood play. I have no doubt that this would not have been achievable without my artistic talents being honed throughout life and education.

The human gifts of imagination, play and creativity have served us for time eternal but it is an unfortunate by-product of human maturation that with time, most people's capacity for creativity steadily decreases. As we grow, learn and gain an understanding of the way ourselves and the world works via experience, education and observation; we become far more fixed in the way we perceive reality and therefore more limited in our mental malleability. This places natural ceilings on our minds that restrict access to the furthest reaches of our respective imaginations.

Upon first listen (or read) this sounds like a fair trade off: 'As I get older I will become wiser, smarter and more solid in my perception of the world but I won't be as playful and imaginative as I was when I was six years old. Fair enough, I can accept that.' However, there are other consequences to this loss of creative and imaginative potential that bear thinking about: we can become less open minded, deeply inhibited, less expressive, and less curious. This is where arts education plays its crucial role in our development.

The arts are imperative because engagement and participation in the arts keeps the mind free, inventive, curious and ensures our minds are always expanding. It is through art that human beings have managed to express the intangible and phenomenal elements of our existence. Through a single melodic progression, humans are able to express emotions so nuanced that no word can accurately define them. Through a single dance move to the groove of a drum pattern, we can ignite a fire in our souls. Through a single brush stroke of colour, we can stir within us feelings of profundity and through the combination of words alone we can achieve the numinous.

Arts subjects such as music, drama, art and English strengthened my innate ability to articulate, appreciate and achieve the intangible through expression. I remember going to school with feelings of anxiety or doubt and then learning about African American blues music and realising that there were these 80-year-old chord progressions through which I could channel and almost release those emotions. I will never forget my amazement when I first encountered pointillism in art classes and learnt how to capture the fragmented quality of memories in the mind and translate them (in their fragmented state) onto a blank canvas using a particular paint brush technique. What the above did was deepen my sense of wonderment for the world both around me and inside me.

This was especially important for me as a Black youth and for Black youths worldwide. As Black people, we have had so much taken away from us in terms of our history and our identity but one thing that can never be removed from us is our artistic expression. It exists within us and it is through education that we can learn to appreciate it and access it, thereby deepening our sense of cultural identity. I had guitar lessons in primary school in which we were taught classical music but growing up in a Nigerian household and discovering the virtuoso Nigerian guitarist King Sunny Ade did more to enthuse me than any European classical piece that I was taught. Naturally, I felt inspired to invent and attempt things I'd never even considered on guitar once I heard how this instrument was interpreted by a legend from my own culture. Reading a book by a Nigerian writer such as Wole Soyinka or Chinua Achebe undoubtedly revealed more to me about who I am as an African man than any book by a white novelist. There is the obvious fact that I felt represented when I read books which featured characters from my own culture but there is also the familiarity of phrasing, cultural references and that intangible thing we call essence. When absorbing books from writers of the African Diaspora, I was able to tap into elements of my being and consciousness that books by white writers simply didn't give me the pathways to. Furthermore, if students from other cultures are exposed to more diverse literature and arts in general, it encourages multicultural harmony in ways that merely living alongside each other cannot truly achieve.

Culturally speaking, art is psycho-emotional transference. This is to say that whenever we create anything, we have essentially created a time capsule of our thoughts and feelings at the time of creation which those who are then exposed to it will then receive. Through the traditions of food, music, art, clothing and language, we are able to communicate so many aspects of our afro-centricity across time. With music, language, art and clothing in particular, we are able to capture not just our psycho-emotional state, cultural connectivity, uniqueness and richness of culture, but also the spirit of the culture and the intangible. So much of what inspires me artistically was given to me via afro-cultural education outside of school. As a child, I was often taken to see Black theatre productions, I watched Nollywood films and grew up in a household in which music from across the African diaspora was played. Through this exposure to art, I was absorbing knowledge, feeling and essence from the African diaspora. In the modern day, I artistically innovate and regurgitate all I've absorbed in my own unique way and therefore contribute to the rich and circular, time-transcendent tapestry that is Black art. Through education, so many kids who were not fortunate enough to be exposed to Black art in the way that I was will have the opportunity to discover parts of themselves that may only be partially within reach without it... or in the worst cases: not reachable at all. If one is not able to reach these parts of themselves, existentially speaking, who's to say they will ever reach their most authentic version of self?

As humans, we are not bound by instinct as most animals are; we have the gift of abstract thought which is the ability to consider concepts beyond what we physically observe. The ability to recognise patterns, dissect ideas, process information, problem solve and create things all involve and require abstract thinking. We live in a world in which art quite literally surrounds us. Every building, car, advert, light, song, film, book and all else that we create began as an idea or more specifically as a thought. Through arts education, we develop ourselves as abstract thinkers, as problem solvers, as expressers of the human condition and expressers of the intangible. When we educate Black youths in art from across the African diaspora, we deepen their investment in their culturally unique creative capacity and we give them a sense of ownership and belonging in this ever sprawling universe. Through Black arts education, we show all Black children that they can manifest their ideas into reality. We show them that the achievement of their dreams is entirely feasible as would be proven by the wealth of art they would be exposed to and educated in. The arts enrich the experience of learning during one's school years as well as preparing students for life beyond school. Arts subjects encourage independent thought, confidence in expression and creativity. It is true that as we grow older we drift further from that childlike state of unlimited creativity and curiosity, but it is through the arts that we are able to hold onto it and use it not merely as a child who is at the mercy of their whims but as an adult who is able to critically think and utilise these intangible gifts to better understand the world around us and the world within us.

Chioma Ezeh – The privatisation and erosion of arts

Chioma is a London-based product designer and storyteller, having worked across theatre and film, both behind and in front of the camera. Her debut short film, 'Behind the Door', kick-started her entry into the industry, garnering audiences both domestically and internationally. She's passionate about artistry, creative development and representation.

In many ways, creative subjects were a lifeline for me. At its core, schooling can resemble a sort of conveyor belt; moving you quickly through the processes of assignments, keeping up appearances and meeting expectations. At times, these pressures were crippling. Creative subjects were a sort of solitude, my respite amongst the chaos.

Upon leaving education, it becomes significantly easier to connect the dots. You grow to realise there's an undercurrent that underpins public schooling and if you aren't given the opportunity to find your rhythm within it, you're left behind. This undercurrent is the life force of many public education systems; the ones I've personally experienced as well as those discovered through my own professional career – perhaps as a byproduct or the sole aim entirely; prioritises attainment above all else; leaving any efforts to cultivate and maintain teacher and student community by the wayside.

Interestingly, I discovered that the confidence I gained in creative subjects leant itself across the majority of my core curriculum. Essentially, these subjects were my gateway into finding what worked for me, allowing me to find my own rhythm. School no longer felt like a task in endurance. In fact, it allowed me to embrace a sense of duality – where I discovered that I could be surprisingly competent at two totally unrelated subjects, rather than ascribe to this singularity of what success looked like.

What I began to enjoy most about school was this synergy – the mass exodus of pupils from maths class in the pursuit of often vastly different territories. Depending on the timetable, it may have been drama or a textiles class where instead of rulers and equations, the tools were canvases, oil paints and rich fabrics I had sourced the weekend before from the uncles in Tooting market. The room always felt alive, welcoming unique perspectives and interpretation. I'd present research and the many (at times questionable) physical attempts to interpret the work of artists such as Issey Miyake and Kara Walker, two artists who embraced distinct *avant garde* approaches within their creations. Much like with maths and science, I could exit the classroom a vastly different person, changed simply through the discovery of something new – experiences that have aided my varied career within storytelling and tech.

Despite this improvement, there existed a culture of systems and narratives that could feel dispiriting. The community of Black girls, now women, with careers and families of their own, were an intrinsic part of my development. However, this appreciation was not always apparent amongst our educators. I remember what felt like a distinct contrast between our experiences versus those of our peers. Coupled with the over-representation of Black and Brown pupils across the lower education sets, it meant that this disparity existed on a psychological scale too. In many ways, our sets felt indicative of the expectations our educators held for us, and could govern how wide we dared to cast our aspirations.

Having worked in schools, I can appreciate the benefits of education sets. It allows teachers and educators alike to tailor information and better cater to the varying needs of a set of pupils, in cases where sometimes the only similarity amongst them is their age. When this becomes detrimental is in those cases where ranking is weaponised – imposing a culture of self-limiting beliefs, encouraging teachers to disregard competencies that general testing cannot screen for. When you're both Black and from a lower socio-economic background, chances are you are well aware of the status quo – inequalities, disparaging narratives, a lack of opportunities and genuine representation. When schools perpetuate this, it's always a tragedy.

I was fortunate to have some adults on my side who championed my growth and encouraged me to push beyond limitations, my drama teacher being one of them. I distinctly recall a time when he asked each one of us 'what grade we wanted to achieve'. It was the first time a teacher had ever invited me to actively participate in my own attainment. And perhaps, for many students, it was a chance to engage without imposed ceilings.

Given the pressures and cuts to funding, it's understandable many educators are struggling to prioritise student access to creativity. In February 2022, the UK government announced its decision to crack down on loan provisions for 'low-value degrees', prompting sentiments that creative degrees simply weren't worth the investment (see, for example, Davis, 2022; Smith, 2022; Spier, 2022). While my focus here is within secondary education, it's easy to see how these beliefs trickle down – establishing a culture that disregards creativity but in the same breath wouldn't function the same without it. Within these environments, students learn skills such as teamwork, the practice of ideation, a lived under-standing of work ethic and perseverance and, importantly, that success isn't singular. Rather, success is a personal achievement that, along with introspection, they can learn to define for themselves. When we open up this channel, we're more likely to build students who are better equipped for adulthood and the pressures that await beyond the classroom.

'Everybody is a genius. But if you judge a fish by its ability to climb a tree, it will live its whole life believing that it is stupid' is a well-known quote, popularly attributed to Albert Einstein, but one that I think perfectly encapsulates the result of a *one-size-fits-all* curriculum. When we remove or downplay the role of crea-tive subjects, we end up isolating students whose genius may lie dormant across core subjects. When entry to the arts is absent within mainstream schooling, it reduces the options young people and their families can access. Beyond this, the majority of external initiatives exist behind costly paywalls. With the cost of living crisis and financial pressures increasing, these options may be out of the question for some families, which may explain the culture of underrepresentation across the creative industries. The less mainstream inclusion there is, the further we perpetuate the privatisation of creativity.

References

Davis, A. (2022) Clampdown on 'Mickey Mouse' degrees in major funding overhaul. *Evening Standard*, 23 February [online]. www.standard.co.uk/news/education/universities-degrees-higher-education-grades-funding-student-loans-b984218.html (accessed 4 November 2022).

Smith, S. (2022) The government plans to scrap student loans for 'Mickey Mouse' degrees. *Dazed*, 19 January [online]. www.dazeddigital.com/life-culture/article/55259/1/the-government-plans-to-scrap-student-loans-for-mickey-mouse-degrees (accessed 4 November 2022).

Spier, S. (2022) Cracking down on 'Mickey Mouse degrees' isn't the answer. *The Times*, 9 February [online]. www.thetimes.co.uk/article/cracking-down-on-mickey-mouse-degrees-isnt-the-answer-tcbntkphr (accessed 4 November 2022).

Big questions

I think the question is less 'what return on our investment can we get out of this?' and rather 'how many opportunities are we giving our students to experience success within education?' In my experience, young people can often feel disenfranchised when those entrusted to guide them fail to account for subjective measures of excellence and talent. This is particularly crucial for students who are neurodiverse, for example.

My suggestion for educators would be to take a moment to review the status quo of their learning environments; to question whether depictions and narratives around success and what counts as a celebratory achievement are inclusionary or exclusionary.

Whose experience is prioritised within the curriculum?

- **'Core versus creative'**: Explore your own preconceptions around creative and core education subjects, questioning whether any of these need to be reviewed. Consider how you might help advocate for more positive dialogues and perspectives surrounding creative subjects/career paths.
- **Concrete ceilings versus achievement**: Critically assess the practical application of sets within your classroom – is the language around these groupings uplifting or demoralising? How can you ensure that students across lower sets capitalise on their skills and experience self-efficacy, and similarly, that they aren't deterred by perceived limitations?
- **On advocacy**: Consider whether students are encouraged to advocate their needs, particularly those who may be falling behind, have SEN or are neurodiverse. Their insight may just surprise you.
- **Personalising the curriculum**: Consider how you can stimulate student participation within attainment. Ask students what they would like to gain from their lessons – perhaps translating these into the form of personal goals students may feel hold more meaning for them.
- **Co-opting what works**: For students who strive in creative settings, investigate the techniques you can co-opt or increase within core subject settings.
- **Hope and a plan**: Are these students provided with opportunities to help them plan towards and successfully pursue creative careers?
- **Notes on ethos**: What is your classroom's ethos? What aspirations do you have for your students and how does this translate within the time you spend with them?

Index